SCENARIO SELLING

TECHNOLOGY AND THE FUTURE
OF PROFESSIONAL SELLING

Patrick J. Sullivan and
Dr. David L. Lazenby

SCENARIO PUBLICATIONS

SCENARIO PUBLICATIONS

Order this book online at www.trafford.com
or email orders@trafford.com

Most Trafford titles are also available at major online book retailers.

Cover Design by Steve Cox
Illustrations by Steve Cox, Dan Smith, and Patrick Sullivan

Print information available on the last page.

ISBN: 978-1-4120-3620-7 (sc)
ISBN: 978-1-4122-2740-7 (e)

Trafford rev. 03/31/2022

 www.trafford.com

North America & international
toll-free: 844-688-6899 (USA & Canada)
fax: 812 355 4082

C O N T E N T S

Part IV: The Future of Selling

Afterward

PREFACE

WHAT IS THIS BOOK ABOUT?

"An invasion of armies can be resisted, but not an idea whose time has come."
—Victor Hugo, from 'Histoire d'un crime.' 1852

This is a book about professional selling—what salespeople do with and for customers—and how it's changing due to advances in technology. Since 1997 my business partner and co-author, Dr. David Lazenby, Ph.D., and I have studied how technology has historically altered successful sales tools and methods. This book is the result of that research. Readers will gain an understanding of the changes required for salespeople and the selling profession to survive and thrive in the Digital Age.

The development and widespread use of Digital-Age technologies has resulted in and continues to introduce significant changes in the way people live, work, learn, *buy, and sell.*

Will technology eliminate the need for salespeople?

Within these pages you'll discover why today's Digital-Age technologies may well replace many salespeople; and be introduced to perhaps the only sales method and tool-set that will make salespeople irreplaceable: ScenarioSelling[SM].

Those who follow this system will create real value for their customers, build stronger customer relationships, gain a competitive advantage, and thrive. Those who don't may lose out to competitors who will.

Are you willing to be influenced to improve the way that you sell? If not, read no further. If you are, welcome and read on. We hope you find the ideas and examples inside interesting and valuable.

WHAT IS SCENARIOSELLING?

ScenarioSelling merges high-tech tools and a high-touch process to create *just-in-time* (fast) *professional selling*. It results in a significant reduction in the time required for complex decisions and sales, which can be reduced to hours rather than weeks or months.

ScenarioSelling isn't a new sales technique…*it's a new sales process*. It represents the first major change in sales process since consultative selling was introduced over 40 years ago. ScenarioSelling provides the logic and framework for a whole new way of selling—a model that will surpass the current paradigm of consultative selling in productivity, personal touch, and professionalism. As a result, the ideas we're proposing represent a fundamentally different way to plan and sell with technology that flies in the face of conventional wisdom, training, and tools in the sales training industry.

Are we suggesting then that these concepts are radical, unproven, and unscientific? NO! While the ideas that you'll see here may be new to sales professionals, they are already established as best practices in many other business disciplines.

ScenarioSelling is based on the same practical and proven scientific principles of: Accelerated Learning; Lean Thinking; Just-in-Time; Process Re-engineering; Simulation; Scenario Planning; and Systems Thinking that revolutionized American manufacturing and marketing practices during the 1980's and 1990's.

This combination of high-tech efficiency and high-touch professionalism also results in:

- Shorter sales cycles
- Significantly increased sales productivity (sales effectiveness and efficiency)
- A dramatically different and better sales experience for prospects and clients
- Differentiation and a tremendous edge over traditional competition

So...How Do You Do It?

In the ScenarioSelling process, customers and salespeople work together using visual-interactive technologies (like computers, multimedia projectors, and specially designed visual software programs) to identify issues, solve problems, and make decisions in real time. The following table summarizes what this looks like and how it differs from a traditional consultative sales approach.

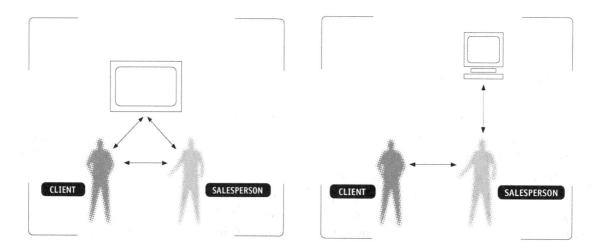

ScenarioSelling Approach	Traditional Approach
Technology used with the customer	Technology used away from customer
Technology designed to facilitate visual interactive work and play	Technology designed to create printouts and static slideshow presentation
Think 'flight simulator'	Think 'report generator'
It's a Collaborative Process: "Let's do it together."	It's a Consultative Process: "I'll do it for you."
Changes and new information can be made quickly and new results shown instantly	Changes and new information require do-overs and extra meetings
Sales Role: Process Facilitator	*Sales Role*: Information/Technical 'Expert' Resource

How Does It Work?

ScenarioSelling works by eliminating the inevitable delays that result from using backroom analysis software and technology tools with a consultative selling process. Most of these productivity draining and sales killing delays are not necessary. They are simply the result of how customer decisions and consultative selling break down when backroom planning and report preparation tools (tools used away from the customer) are used as part of the sales process.

The picture below helps illustrate the problem and the solution. The blocks summarize the different activity groups (events) that take place during the sales process. Block #1 (Rapport & Interview) and Block #3 (Demonstrate & Implement) are customer-facing events. However, Analysis (Block #2) is not. When Analysis is needed that requires the salesperson to be away from the client to complete it, the flow of the sale process is interrupted and additional time or meetings are required.

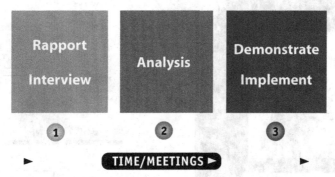

So, any additions or changes (like new information that a client introduces at the time of presentation or client questions that the salesperson hasn't prepared for) require analysis 'do-overs'…adding meetings…delaying decisions…and killing sales.

What's the solution to the sales delay and do-over problem illustrated above? *Close the loop with visual tools that allow analysis to be completed while you're with the prospect.* Is ScenarioSelling as simple as taking a laptop or computer screen and turning it around during the sales process so the customer can see the analysis software being used? While this is a good start, it's not enough, because the type of interaction that takes place also requires a different process and different skills than those used in traditional consultative selling.

It's collaborative not consultative! What's required to facilitate this collaboration? Imagine the types of tools and skills that would be required if you used computer software as a visual flight simulator to help customers navigate their way through difficult decisions…

ScenarioSelling is like 'decision flight simulation' with the prospect or client as the student pilot and the salesperson as flight instructor.

⭐ ## From the Customer's Perspective...

How does ScenarioSelling provide a better customer experience? Let's look at an example from the financial services industry. Imagine for a moment that you're the customer... You're looking for financial advice and someone who can help you achieve your dreams and goals. Take a look at the picture below. Which sales experience would *you* rather go through?

The collaborative ScenarioSelling process results in a profoundly different and better customer experience than other professional selling methods because it:
- Increases customers involvement and participation in the sales process
- Helps people see their thinking illustrated in real time, allows them to talk about it, and gets people on the same page
- Engages people's imagination and helps them dream productively
- Encourages risk taking, experimentation, and sharing of ideas
- Makes the process productive and playful rather than painful and boring
- Helps people get questions answered faster
- Inspires and motivates people to explore issues, solve problems, and make decisions

What It Means for the Sales Person

Now, imagine that you're the salesperson…
What would it mean if your sales process resulted in engaged and involved prospects:
- Who share information openly?
- Who find the sales process interesting, rather than something to be avoided?
- Who are motivated to explore issues and make decisions…faster?
- And are more committed to implement solutions because they helped create them?

Imagine a sales process that would help you:
- Sell both faster and more professionally?
- Make prospecting easier?
- Make service work more profitable?
- Have prospects and clients want to come in?

What would it mean to your sales productivity?

What would it mean to you personally?

The ScenarioSelling methods will help you see more people, sell more to each person, and do it in less time…providing dramatic increases in sales results…while at the same time making the process more personally and professionally satisfying.

Why Not Do It?

Despite the advantages of this approach, there will be many salespeople who either can't or won't be able to do this for reasons including...

- *Change in Behavior.* Ever try to take someone who's successful at something and ask them to start doing it differently? There will be many sales advisors who either can't or won't be able to do this because it will force them to think about selling and do selling differently.
- *Tools, Training, and Skills.* Some of the visual interactive tools required to do this weren't available or easily affordable as recently as a few years ago. Until very recently, the software and training to sell this way easily and effectively haven't existed.
- *Familiarity.* The core ideas in this book including just-in-time, simulation, systems thinking, and scenario planning are concepts that many people are not yet familiar with. We hope to begin resolving the familiarity issues through this book and our training programs.

One of the goals we have for this book is to adequately describe the tools, process, and skills needed for people to implement the ScenarioSelling process easily, effectively, and profitably. In the next section, we describe different ways to use this book to accomplish that goal.

A READER'S GUIDE: HOW SHOULD YOU READ THIS BOOK?

There are four parts to this book that will...

- Provide sales stories that provide the background (Part I—ScenarioSelling Stories)
- Illustrate the problems that salespeople face that current methods and tools cannot solve (Part II—Selling Past & Present)
- Describe the changes necessary to address this issue and meet the new requirements for selling in the Digital Age (Part III—Reengineering the Sales Process)
- Introduce a model that will help you, or your competitor, solve complex customer problems, and sell faster and more effectively—with technology (Part IV—The Future of Selling)

How should you read this book? There are as many different ways to read a book as there are different types of readers. You can skim it, skip around, or read straight through. Most books are designed for linear reading and thinking—chapter-by-chapter, in order, each one building on the chapter before it. But not everyone reads a book straight through from front to back.

This book was built to give you choices in how you read it and use it:
- Each chapter was written so that it could be a stand-alone article or white paper. So start where you like and read in any order you want.
- Every chapter was also designed following a template for professional presentations so that they could be delivered in a classroom environment. The intent was to make it easier for people to learn by helping them see how it could be explained to other people.

Because we took this approach, there is some intentional repetition, although we've tried to eliminate as much duplication as possible. However you like to read, we hope the book's design helps you do it productively.

So where should you start? We suggest a couple of different possible paths depending on whether your learning objective is:

- Getting a basic idea of what ScenarioSelling is (recognition)
- A deeper look that will help you talk about it and explain it to others (understanding)
- To be able to do it (implementation)
- To master it and even help us improve it (integration)

Generally speaking, Part I provides the background, using stories and examples; Part II describes the 'what'; Part III describes the 'why'; and Part IV describes the 'how'. So, if you want to understand the entire concept and how to apply it, you should read the entire book. You can read it in the traditional way—front to back—Parts I-IV, in order. But here are a couple alternative approaches to get the most out of this book for the time you put in.

"I Want a Quick Read"

If you only have 15 minutes to read or you just want a high level overview, go straight to Chapter 18: ScenarioSelling Summary. This recaps each of the chapters in a few sentences and attempts to bring together all of the concepts in the book.

If you have an hour, read Part I: ScenarioSelling Stories. These are real sales stories that lead to the development of ScenarioSelling. These stories use examples of selling financial services, but the lessons learned can be applied to many different industries.

"I Want a Good Basic Understanding"

The following chapters provide a good basic overview of the key ScenarioSelling concepts:

- Chapter 3: Consultative Selling & Technology—A Tale of WOE
- Chapter 4: Selling—The Next Generation
- Chapter 11: Technology & Selling Reconsidered
- Chapter 12: From Consultative to Collaborative
- Chapter 13: A Learning Approach
- Chapter 15: The ScenarioSelling Model

"Skip the Theory, I Just Want to Do It"

If you just want to do it, read Part III, particularly Chapters 12, 15, 16, and 17. Here we talk about specific skills, techniques, and applications. The stories in Part I may also provide some practical ideas that may be of use to you, for example, the 'Financial Voyeurism' story describes how to use the ScenarioSelling process to facilitate prospecting seminars.

"I Want to Know More About It: What It Is and Why It Works"

Parts II, III, and IV of this book give a formal structure to the discoveries in Part I—the what, the why, and the how of the ScenarioSelling system.

Part I and II provide the background, including a historical framework, to explain why ScenarioSelling is both an inevitable and important step in the evolution of selling.

Part III provides a deeper understanding of the reasoning and the science behind ScenarioSelling. The material is more theoretical and less practitioner-oriented than the other sections. But we believe it's very helpful to understand the science behind it, which makes it very important reading for sales professionals.

Chapters 12, 13, and 14 from Part IV explain the 'Selling as Learning' model and bridge the theories from Part III with selling practice. The college course outline (Appendix) provides additional information that you may find helpful.

"I Have Some Ideas and Experiences I'd Like to Share With Others About This"

We spent the better part of seven years reflecting, connecting, selling, writing, and re-writing to create this book. Despite the time, research, and effort put into this (and maybe because of it), we are aware of and humbled by how imperfect and incomplete it is.

We have already written several new articles that we intend to put into a future edition. And we have also developed many practical tools that further enhance the implementation and teaching of ScenarioSelling that we didn't include in this version.

We have no illusions of this book being the last word on selling. Instead, we hope it's the beginning of a dialogue on selling's next steps. With that in mind, we would appreciate your suggestions, corrections, stories, and proposed additions or deletions so we can update and upgrade this book.

To share your ideas or to learn from the experiences of other sales professionals, visit the ScenarioSelling website at www.scenarioselling.com and subscribe to our newsletter.

We appreciate your interest in our book and we look forward to hearing from you so we can keep the dialogue going.

ACKNOWLEDGEMENTS

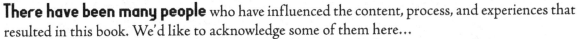

There have been many people who have influenced the content, process, and experiences that resulted in this book. We'd like to acknowledge some of them here…

To Our Families…especially our wives, our children, and our parents, for their love, their support, and their practically unlimited patience. We can't thank you enough.

To Our Clients. To the thousands of users of our sales and software products worldwide, whose recommendations and feedback have proved so valuable to refining the tools and our processes.

To Their Clients. We would not have been able to accomplish this without the early participation, indulgence, and support of hundreds of financial service consumers, who helped us understand that sales advisors could sell more effectively when they stopped teaching and started learning.

To Our Colleagues. Andrew L. Larsen was there at the beginning and encouraged the idea as it evolved from napkin sketches to finished products. Gus Larsen provided 50+ years of top-level sales experience and helped guide our ambitions and objectives with thoughtful mentoring.

Ken Urban, Dick Geach, Scott Dixon, Jill Flickinger, Steve Kroeger, Paul Lindvall, Terri Sandefer, Mike Clark, Mark Rottler, Jeff Hartle, and the management and staff of Grand Premier Financial Services (now part of 5th/3rd Bank). The ScenarioSelling project never would have gotten off the ground without their thoughtful input and support.

The owners of Brentmark Software (Greg Kolojeski, Pat Matthews, and Jane Schuck) and to Keith Reynolds for their talent and commitment that helped turn our RetireNow software from a dream into a reality.

To the entire RSM McGladrey Wealth Management sales team particularly David Pierce, John Moraites, Jay Zack, Bob Eichten, Allen Jacobs, Mark Miskell, and David Klintworth for their valuable input and support, and their commitment to improving the client sales experience.

Other Friends, Contributors, and Supporters Included…William Sullivan, Greg Downey of US Bank, Steve Schepman, Hugo Ernst, and Teresa Probert of First Banks, Mark Knackendoffel of Manhattan Trust Co., Chris Schildz of Commerce Bank, Steven Martin of Key Bank, Alex and Nila Paradowski, Steve Cox, Dan Smith, Bill Ottinger, Charles D. 'Skip' Fox, Charles Lowenhaupt, Ted Elses, J.J. Stupp, SEI's George Tsiaras, Mark Workman, Bert Decker, Kent Heise, Dan Shoemaker, David McMenamin, Tab Hockamier, Jaime Punishill of CapGemini Management, Jeff Bush, Rob Driscoll, William Reilly, Steve Lindstrom, Sunil Puri, Bob Slonim, Craig Ford, Dick Lafontaine, DeWaine Svela, Dr. Lorry Lazenby, Ken Harrington of the The Skandalaris Center for Entrepreneurial Studies at Washington University, Dr. John Grable of Kansas State University, Rob Roderman at the University of Missouri, Dr. Sharon Devaney at Purdue University, and Carol Lee at DePaul University.

*And Last But Definitely Not Least...*To the staff of ScenarioNow Inc., particularly Cindy Larsen and Donna Tiff for their contributions, their dedication, and their belief in us.

I

Part I
INTRODUCTION

Part I
Part I
Part I
Part I

SCENARIOSELLING STORIES

"Innovation doesn't come from within. It comes from without."
—Patrick Sullivan

About the Stories

In spring of 1996, Patrick Sullivan had a serendipitous sales 'accident' that changed the course of our careers and lives. The 'accident' and the intentional repeat performances that it inspired have provided us with many interesting stories—some which we share with you here.

The twelve stories in this section are representative samples of hundreds we've gathered during the last seven years. Most of them are written in the first person, as Pat describes what actually occurred in the client meetings.

These are real stories about sales obstacles and innovations that lead to the development of ScenarioSelling. Each of these stories provided us with valuable lessons and insights about how to identify customer needs and sell more effectively—through the appropriate use of technology.

While these stories describe selling in the financial services industry, the ideas can be applied to almost any sales situation that includes both a salesperson and the use of technology.

The Fumble...and the Recovery

In spring of 1996, I received a phone call from Joan, a 58-year old woman. She and her husband, Mike, were prospects I had completed a financial plan for about two months earlier. Our earlier meetings had resulted in a small sale and the potential for an IRA rollover when they retired in a few years. I could tell by her voice that something was wrong. She sounded scared.

Joan told me that Mike had gone in for routine bypass surgery and had died on the table. She asked if I would come out and review their plan with her. Mike had been handling all of the issues regarding investments and she wasn't even really sure what they had.

She didn't realize it yet, but financially she was going to be fine. Her husband had accumulated over $1 million in his retirement plan at work, and he had a life insurance policy with a $500,000 death benefit. I printed up another financial planning 'book' and drove to her house about an hour from my office.

I opened the planning binder and started to go through it with her. Within a few minutes, she pointed to a figure that she said was wrong. Sure enough, she was right. I had made a simple input error. My mistake. I knew that this wasn't going to change the result or my recommendations, but it cast just enough doubt in her mind to keep her from acting.

I offered to return to my office, reprint the plan with the new figures, and bring it back to her…but she wasn't going to be available again for another two weeks. I tried explaining the issue away. The harder I tried to bail myself out, the deeper the hole got. I was staring at a $500,000 life insurance death benefit check on the table. I had investment account applications and rollover papers in my briefcase filled out and ready to go. And I was beginning to realize that I was going to go home empty handed.

So…I improvised. I offered to go out to my car, get my laptop computer, and fix the issue for her right now…and that I would bring her the printed version later. I brought the computer back in, fired it up, and attempted a save. At this point, we were about 30 minutes into the appointment, but it had seemed like hours.

I made the corrections, pulled up graphs that illustrated the answers, and turned the computer around to show it to her. It answered her initial question, but she quickly came up with another. I turned the computer back toward me, made the changes, and spun it around again. She asked another. This time I didn't turn the computer around. I made the changes while we talked and the two of us looked at it together.

Then something very interesting happened. I saw things I hadn't thought about earlier, so *I* started asking questions. We made the changes and answered them together. This fueled a dialogue that got deeper and deeper into what she really wanted. It took us into places that neither of us had expected to go. I showed her retiring immediately rather than the two years we had initially projected. I showed her gifting to her children and grandchildren. I even showed her buying a winter home in Florida. We were both so totally wrapped up in this that we forgot about the time. We stopped and looked at the clock. Over two hours had passed. But this time it seemed like minutes.

The results of the meeting were equally stunning. She decided to retire immediately. She also decided to visit friends in Florida to consider the suggestion about the winter home. She set up accounts for her grandchildren's college.

I'm not sure who was more surprised, her or me. She got more than what she expected. She had her fears addressed and saw that her dreams were in fact possible. She made life-changing decisions quickly, comfortably, and confidently. I walked out that evening with the $500,000 check and the agreement for the $1 million rollover.

When I drove home that evening, I knew that something significant had happened. There was something substantially different and better about this experience that I hadn't yet figured out how to put into words. Then the light bulb turned on. I pulled off on the side of the road and wrote ½ hours worth of notes…

What happened? I used the computer to recover from a mistake and save a sale.

But how?

- I made a mistake…
- I had to fix it…
- I used the laptop in front of her…
- I made changes with her…
- We didn't need the printouts…
- She got more involved…
- The customer made and implemented decisions that would normally take 3-4 meetings…

*We identified and solved the issues—**together**. I sold more…faster…by doing what I would normally do away from her in front of her…by collaborating with the customer using technology!*

Intriguing! I wanted to see what would happen if I did it on purpose to see if it was just a fluke.

⭐ Mirror…Mirror…On the Wall

I had the next couple come to my office. This time, I decided to rent a projector to make it easier for all three of us to look at. I hooked up the computer and blew up the images on a conference room wall like a big screen TV.

The prospects, a doctor and his wife, were celebrating his recent retirement from a successful family practice. They were looking forward to traveling, winters in Florida, and spending more time with their grandchildren. They had $1.75M between two retirement accounts: one with $1.5 million, the other $250,000. He did all of his own investing and took great pride in the results. Going into the conversation, he made it clear that he intended to manage the majority of the money and was looking for an advisor to manage a small piece (about $250,000).

They also recently visited with their attorney who suggested they consider family gifting to reduce potential estate taxes in the future. They came to me asking what they should gift and how much.

My original intent was simply to show them how to get what they wanted—to illustrate gifting—and hope to get some portion of their investment portfolio to manage as a result.

I reviewed their information ahead of time. It was not at all what I expected. When I ran retirement projections with the data and assumptions they had given me, I showed them running out of money in their 80's. There had to be a mistake. They had a reasonably significant net worth. I double-checked all the entries—no mistakes. As it turns out, there were two problems. (1) Their current lifestyle required $125,000 after taxes. (2) All of their investments were in retirement plans, so that every dollar used for income out was taxable. When you took into account taxes and inflation, there simply wasn't going to be enough.

What would you do in a situation like this? Suppose someone walks into your office and tells you they've recently retired and they're looking for someone to manage $250,000. Is your first instinct to: say 'Yes, we can do that. Please sign this application.' or do you leave the $250,000 on the table and tell them how they're going to run out of money in the hope of getting the whole account? Get the whole account? Not very likely going into this meeting. The doctor even made the point—emphatically—before we even started. *Survey says*...open the $250,000 investment account like the client wants. Do the planning later!

As they arrived, I made the decision to go forward with the 'harsh reality' presentation. Despite the sales risk, I felt it was the right thing to do. But I was really torn. Since they did not know me very well, I felt that by giving them bad news they didn't expect I may be putting the sale and the relationship at risk...especially since they were already 'sure' they'd be OK.

Validation of the information was going to be very important if they were going to give it any credibility. So, to start off, instead of just presenting the results, I decided to walk through the inputs with them so it would be easier to grasp the 'why' behind the 'what.' We looked at the big screen together. I asked them to help me verify the inputs and assumptions, not letting on that I already knew what the outputs looked like.

The mood of the meeting at this point was light and upbeat. They were joking about what they were going to spend and where they were going to travel. Then, I projected the results. The first graph showed their net worth. It looked like a ski slope. I explained to them that this illustrated the value of their total net worth (assets less liabilities) over time and demonstrated that given the current assumptions they, by age 85, would have spent all of their money.

"I don't understand," he said. "I've done my own calculations and the results looked fine. Let's double check the numbers." We checked the interest rates, the account values, inflation, taxes, spending...everything checked out. It was like looking into a technological mirror. It wasn't the story he expected or wanted to see, but it was difficult to deny. The doctor paused and then asked, "Are you telling me that I have to go back to work?"

I responded, "No. It means that given your current assets, projected rates of return, and other assumptions we made here that you will not have enough to support your desired standard of living past age 85."

He turned to his wife and said, very seriously, "Dear...you have to start spending less money." To which she very quickly and pointedly countered, "Well then, you're not going to manage the investments!"

They spent the next two minutes (it seemed like an hour) in an intense personal discussion about her spending and his investment management. After it was over, they turned to me and asked what they could/should do to fix the problem they were looking at. I began to play out scenarios at various levels of spending to determine what they could afford without changing their investment strategy. Then I started illustrating the type of return necessary to meet various spending targets. We watched the results play out as possible life stories on the wall. These visual scenarios helped facilitate a very intense discussion on the tradeoffs between spending and rates of return and how to get what they *both* wanted.

Then he asked, "What would you do with the money if *you* invested it?" I showed him various alternatives for restructuring his portfolio to reduce his risk and increase return. I tweaked his plan to try and provide a good balance of desired income with reasonable investment objectives. Each successive scenario got closer, while pulling out their thoughts, and involving them in the process.

We created a scenario with reasonable assumptions that showed their investments lasting until age 90. The doctor looked straight at me and said, "If you can help us achieve **that,** I'm willing to let you manage the $1.5M, and I'll manage the $250,000. I just need to manage enough to stay involved."

I closed the sale on the $1.5 million investment account...without ever generating a printed plan.

Two prospects...two accounts...over $3 million in investments. I had now blown past curiosity. I knew I was on to something, but I hadn't quite figured out what yet. The next meeting provided a big clue.

It's Not About the Presentation... It's About the Interview!

It was a quarter to five, when one of my business associates walked into my office. He told me that one of his clients had heard about the 'computer thing' we were doing from a doctor at the country club. "I know this is an unusual request, but this guy has all of his information with him. Can you come over and do it...right now?"

I was a little surprised. I wasn't used to the idea of people walking in with their information and asking me to do a plan for them. And I was going to have to do the entire thing on the fly. I usually had the customer's information ahead of time, so I could enter it, look at it, think about it, and come up with a 'presentation.' This was going to be a new challenge for me. But since it was a warm call on his existing client, I thought I'd try it.

I carried the equipment down to the other advisor's office and set it up. It took me about 5 minutes to set up the laptop and projector. I had a printed factfinder next to me, but I decided to try inputting the information directly into the software as I asked the questions to save time. The meeting went very well. Although it didn't result in any new business for me, going through the entire planning process 'live' taught me several important lessons:

It Was Easier than I Expected. Gathering the information 'on the fly' wasn't awkward at all. In fact, there were certain advantages...

It Didn't Take More Time, It Took Significantly Less Time. A normal thorough interview, the traditional way, would have taken me roughly an hour. Then I would have to go away to put the data into software...to perform analysis, do printouts, etc. And then, wait a week or longer 'til the next meeting to begin discussing results and possibilities. In this interview, we entered the data and were looking at results and possibilities within the first 30 minutes.

No Validation Required. Even when I entered data and prepared analysis ahead of time, I normally would end up spending 30 minutes validating the inputs with the clients. This is necessary, in most cases, because fitting the client's numbers into a software program usually requires consolidating them or renaming them to fit the 'boxes' in the program. Since this may not be the way clients think about them, unless properly identified and explained, it can introduce confusion and doubt (and reduces trust). But...when I did it with the client—they helped put the numbers in. I didn't have to validate my entries. The clients 'owned' them.

Recovery. I also learned that the ability to recover was more important than having the right answers to start with! Fumbling and making mistakes wasn't a problem. In fact, when the client saw a mistake, he pointed it out. He fixed it. So the numbers were *right*...even further validating them.

Better Information. My friend told me that he had been working with this client for over 10 years, but that he learned more about him during this meeting than ever before. He even learned about accounts with other sales advisors he had never been told about. He ended up selling a $150,000 annuity as a result.

Then I recognized, *"I'm not using this just as a presentation tool…I'm using it as an interview tool."* I was getting better, deeper information about client facts, concerns, and assumptions faster…because instead of feeling probed, the client was getting instant rewards for providing it.

Technology-enabled collaboration…
A technological mirror…
A technology-enhanced interview that yielded more and better information without having to have all the information up front…
Someone actually heard about it and came in and asked me to do it…

And I was able to do the whole thing from front to end in one meeting by using the software to interview the client. I didn't realize yet the full implications of this, but I made a significant decision. From now on, I would attempt to do them all this way (start to finish in one meeting).

The pieces were starting to come together.

Why Do We Need Another Meeting?

Bob and Yvonne were looking for help. Bob was tired of the corporate game. After 30 years as an insurance executive, he was ready to retire. Yvonne supported the move. But they weren't sure if they could afford it. Bob was 61, ten years older than Yvonne. He was sure that she would outlive him and was very concerned that she would be adequately taken care of after he was gone. They needed help evaluating pension options…to see if they could retire now.

I input their data as I interviewed them, and then pulled up the graphic results. Their assumed choice was to select the pension option with the highest guarantee (and lowest payout.) Financial projections with this choice showed them running out of money at their desired lifestyle in retirement. They seemed resigned to the fact that Bob would work two more years.

So I asked them, "What if you selected the higher pension amount? Let's see what would happen." I made the changes needed. It appeared at the higher (life only) pension amount, they could retire immediately.

Bob said, "That's great if I live. But if I die, what will happen to Yvonne?"

"It depends on when you die," I commented. We ran a series of scenarios to look at alternatives. If Bob lived to 90, no problem. 80? No problems. 70? She'd be OK. "But what if I retire today and I died tomorrow?" That scenario didn't look very good—for either of them.

I suggested seeing how much more money they needed to make the problem go away. We ran a few more scenarios and found that it would take less than $300,000. With an additional $300k, it didn't matter financially if Bob died the day after retiring. Yvonne would not have to take a step down in standard of living, regardless of the pension option selected. "But how are we going to come up with an additional $300,000?" they asked. I suggested we look at life insurance since the additional money wasn't going to be necessary unless Bob died. But because of health concerns, including a heart attack, Bob would be difficult (and expensive) to insure. It didn't seem a viable option.

"What can you tell me about your benefits at work?" I asked. I suggested that Bob call the benefits department at his company on his cell phone... during the meeting. It turned out that he could continue his group term until age 70. So I re-ran the scenarios for Bob dying with the insurance in place. It worked. I summarized, "If you continue the group term and select the higher pension payout, you can meet your retirement objectives and protect Yvonne, even if you died tomorrow."

They were thrilled. Then came the words every advisor dreads: "Before we decide what we're going to do, we have to meet with another person who is a friend of ours. He is an advisor with (*a well known top 10 financial company*). We're going to meet with him in two days to review the plan he put together. We'll call you next week and let you know our decision."

I thought to myself, "How did you let this happen?" I kicked myself for not finding out about the other person sooner. I thanked them for their time and told them I looked forward to hearing from them. I assumed that I had lost the prospect.

I got a call next week as promised. Bob and Yvonne wanted to meet with me again. When we sat down, I asked them, "How did your other meeting go?"

They looked at each other and laughed. "There was no comparison. He prepared a nice binder with printouts, but when we started asking him questions about changing pension options, and the other things we talked about, he couldn't answer them. In fact, he proceeded to tell us why this was not a good idea. When it became apparent to him that we needed answers to questions he wasn't prepared for, he suggested that we schedule another meeting. I asked him why we needed another meeting. He said he wanted to review the information and prepare some new illustrations for us. We told him we'd get back to him. We've made our decision. We'd like to sign up to work with you."

Reflections: This was the first time I grasped the real competitive advantage the 'do it now' approach could provide.

Real-time professional selling! When you have tools and a process that help you take a real-time approach to planning, it doesn't just save hours; *it saves meetings* without compromising the quality of the solution. This makes it very difficult for someone to compete against you.

It also begs a great question. When you have the client's attention *now*, why send them away and then try and set up another meeting? Who are the extra meetings for—the client or the advisor?

Show Me the Money—Planning at the Speed of Sight

Dr. Z was a 63 year old emergency room physician. Working as an ER doctor was physically draining between the constant stress and the middle of the night calls. His accountant and wife were telling him he should retire. He continued to work for several reasons, most important being that his job helped fund their missionary work. (He and his wife were missionaries who spend several months per year overseas.) They planned to leave again in a few months, so he came in wanting to see if he could retire…next year.

Dr Z. had accumulated over $2M inside of his retirement plan. He and Mrs. Z lead a relatively frugal lifestyle. Their home was paid for. They spent about $50-60,000 per year after taxes. When I met them, Bob, their CPA came with them. As I gathered their information, I built a profile and projected the results on the wall with the laptop projector.

Instead of him retiring a year from now, I decided to start out by showing him retiring *now*. I figured that if he wanted me to go back, it would be no problem making the change.

I showed them a graph of their 'Net Worth Over Time'—it kept going up. It clearly illustrated that they were not going to run out of money, even if he retired today. A barrage of questions followed. "Does that take into account taking out money to live on?" he asked. "And inflation?" Then he leaned forward over the table and said, "Right now I know where my next paycheck is coming from. When I quit working, that's going to stop. *So, where's my paycheck going to come from in retirement?*"

Then I showed him a 'Cash Flow Over Time' graph: a graphic picture of how much they would spend year to year and where it was going to come from. This graph showed:
- How much would come from social security for both he and his wife
- How much would have to come from investments and retirement savings
- That when they turned 70½ the minimum distributions they would actually have to take from their retirement plan would give them more income than they were going to spend… and they would either spend it or reinvest it

I even showed them spending additional money for their missionary work and where it might come from without putting their financial security at risk.

After this, he summed it up for all of us. "What you're telling us is that I could retire today at the same standard of living we have now…and that our level of wealth will not go down. You're saying that between social security and our savings I not only can replace my paycheck, but we could spend more than we are now. We'd be OK—without me having to go back to work? And… we wouldn't have to give up our missionary work either?"

I simply said, "Yes." He turned to his wife and said, "Well…that was easy!" I shifted our discussion to how the money would be managed and closed a $2,000,000 IRA rollover account.

The CPA nearly fell out of his chair. After the meeting, he told me that he had been *telling* the doctor this same story for two years...but could never get him to act.

Reflections: This case gave me a new understanding of the power of visual media. Everybody is familiar with the saying "Seeing is believing." But why?

In one of my conversations with Dr. Lazenby, I asked him to explain this from a scientific perspective. He told me, "All decisions, even logical ones, are rooted in emotion and the fastest most effective route to people's emotional pathway is visual. I like to tell people it's because the visual pathway has the greatest bandwidth to the brain...so visual messages get through faster. That's why when you're trying to explain answers to the difficult questions people face in retirement—you can't simply tell them, you have to show them."

Bob took a rational and verbal approach to the problem. And he thoroughly explained it. But Dr. Z. was not adequately motivated by logic or listening. In this case, no amount of conversation was going to persuade him to act.

What kind of visual experience was I providing before I started doing this? The same as everybody else. Size 12 type on 8½" x 11" pages while I tried to talk them through decisions!

From now on, I was going to facilitate the client's decision process visually and try to create a financial 'theater' experience.

Planning as 'Serious Play'

Another interesting lesson took place when I met with Alan S., a 48-year-old attorney, in a practice with three other lawyers. He had been there for almost 20 years. He was married with two children. His wife Terri, a teacher, was not with him today. I entered his financial data into the software as we talked. It turned out as we talked that he was considering leaving the practice. He was getting burned out and he felt handcuffed to his career. He wanted me to show him illustrations for early retirement. Retirement at age 60 was reasonable, 55 was a stretch, and 50 out of the question. Well, at least now he knew! He was thankful for the illustrations, but you could tell it wasn't what he wanted to see.

Nothing I had said so far had inspired or motivated him to move any business to me. The meeting (and possibly the relationship) could have ended right there...then I asked him, "Alan, what do you *really* want? I mean, if you could walk away and start over...what would you want to do?"

He looked astonished and said, "I'm not sure. No one has ever asked me that before." After a moment, he started. "I think I'd like to move back home to Kansas, and buy a small farm. And I'd like to go to graduate school, get a master's degree in history, and possibly teach at a college. I love

Civil War history. I'm actively involved in re-enactments around the country."

I was fascinated by the story and the passion he had for it. "Would you like to see if you could do it? Right now!" For the next hour, we played out scenarios to see if it was possible. "How would you generate income until you got your degree? Will this be enough to provide for your lifestyle? Will you need to draw from your investments or retirement plan?" We worked together like we were teammates playing a game…strategizing and trying every angle to see what would ultimately lead us to victory.

We discovered that if they could survive for three years on his wife's salary—plus rents from two properties they owned—he could have the degree behind him. Then if they didn't draw on their retirement plan until age 60…it would work. Alan was thrilled. He had played out his dream and found it was possible.

The most interesting part of this for me was seeing that knowing he could do it was almost as important as actually carrying out the plan. Knowing he could do it empowered him and released him of the burden of obligation. He didn't have to stay in his practice—whether he did or not was now his choice! In fact, he chose to stay in the practice, confident now not just in his accomplishments, but his possibilities and dreams…and I earned the business for both his personal and corporate retirement plans in the process.

Reflections: I had 'graduated' from using the technology just for recovery, data gathering, and presentation. I was starting to play productively. Using the computer interactively with clients and prospects was allowing me to explore ideas and play out possibilities they hadn't even considered… and to help them identify new goals and redefine their dreams.

This 'thing' I was doing was like a game. Not a simple child's game, but a strategy game. It was *serious play*…with a result that was meaningful, valuable, and entertaining!

Financial Voyeurism...Now That's Entertainment!

Over the years, I've done a lot of prospecting seminars on a variety of topics. I've found them a good way to open doors to new relationships and to keep my name and face in front of people. But they're not without their challenges…the costs can be high…people don't always show up…and converting them from seminar attendees to 1:1 appointments can be difficult…

I had an upcoming seminar planned. I became intrigued with the idea of showing people what we were doing—using the laptop and projector to illustrate playing out retirement scenarios. It was working well in 1:1…why not a seminar? I decided to present a hypothetical case and show people what they would get if they came in for an individual appointment. This WYSIWYG (What You See Is What You Get) approach was extremely successful. The conversion rate (number of people who set up meetings as a result) was extremely high. Over the next three years, I did 20+ seminars and over 70% of those that attended set up 1:1 meetings. So I'm going to explain what we did and learned in the process.

The Setup:

- A typical setting would be in a meeting room that would seat 20-30 people.
- I hooked up an LCD projector and a laptop computer and presented on a large screen.
- I arranged tables so everyone could see the screen.
- The presentation would last for approximately one hour and then we'd have lunch.

Before each seminar started, I walked around the crowd and introduced myself to people. Just before we began, I picked out a sample case that I thought might be representative of the people who were in the audience. (I had a couple of different ones prepared.)

During the first 5 minutes, I'd describe to people that this wasn't just a typical seminar; this was a peek into how we work with people; that today we were going to look at a sample based on a real couple...getting to take a look at what somebody else did with their money. I like to call it financial voyeurism. (I have come to understand that for many people the most powerful way for them to learn is by watching what other people do.) I told them that if they came in to see us that this is the sort of thing they would see.

Then I spend about 5 minutes giving a background on the sample client, describing their situation including age, goals, what types of investments they had, etc.

After I finished reviewing the data, I said, *"Before we move on and see the results of the plan... how you think these people are doing?"* This approach created a real sense of personal interest and drama because:

- The case was often similar to theirs.
- In most cases people don't know the answers.

Then I would explain...*"We're going to look at where these people stand today and then look at what they can do and see what they can have."*

To keep the seminar short and to the point, I focused on graphs that answer three questions everybody has about living in retirement:

- 'Are they going to have enough?' Net Worth
- 'Where's the income going to come from to provide their retirement?' Cash Flow
- 'Who's going to get what's left after they're gone?' Wealth Transfer

After we see what their current financial situation looks like, we determine if these people were going to be OK, and identify what their primary issues might be...then the real fun begins.

I ask people questions that introduce possible changes and play out the scenarios that result while they're watching:

- How much do you think these people can spend?
- What will it take to drive them broke? Let's do it and see.
- How much are they going to pay in taxes?
- Should they gift to their kids? What happens if they do? Will they need the money and regret their decision?
- Should we crash the market? What would happen if their largest asset went down in value by 10%? 20%?
- Let's take their largest investment and change the interest rate by .5%; by 1%; what kind of difference does it make?
- If either of them required long-term care...what would happen? Would their retirement plan be in trouble? If so, when?

"Let's just do it and see what happens!"

In each of the scenarios that I ran, I would illustrate potential opportunities and potential problems; show what could cause them; and then fix it. This approach makes for a very lively Q&A. People really get into this. With the range of questions covered, I know I've covered at least one or two major points that every person in the room was wondering about for themselves.

It's fun watching people in the room because, inevitably, I'd see couples turn to each other and start talking. Whenever this happened I knew they were going to come in for an individual meeting.

I'd play out scenarios until the end of the hour, which always seemed to go too fast. Then I always ended by saying...

"We've seen what the financial scenarios for John and Mary (our sample couple) looked like. What would it look like if *your* numbers were in here?

- How much can you spend?
- How much can you gift? Should you gift?
- Can you live better than you are now?
- Would you like to see the scenarios that are most likely to cause trouble for you?

If you make an appointment and come in, I'll walk you through the same process we went through here and send you home with a roadmap to retirement success."

Then we'd adjourn to lunch. During lunch I'd go around to each table and talk to people, give them business cards, get their names, ask them to fill out an evaluation form, and ask them to let me know if they want this done for them.

Reflections: As I mentioned earlier, the conversion rates using this seminar approach were extremely high! As I reflected on it, here is why I thought we had so much success:

- By using the computer to engage people, I kept their attention.
- I didn't send them home with answers, I sent them home with questions.
- The range of questions addressed covered issues that were relevant for everyone in the room.
- I demonstrated that they were questions I could answer.
- Everybody wants to see what their financial situation 'looks like.'
- When they come in, they knew what I was going to do and what they were going to go through because the seminar gave them a test drive.
- They could see that this style of planning would make the process interesting and fun, rather than boring and painful.

Interesting? Fun? Not boring and painful? Is this planning we're talking about here? What we're doing here is a form of entertainment. Planning as entertainment? I had never thought of it this way before. For most people, the planning/sales process is a lousy entertainment experience. It's like spending all afternoon with a boring relative who tries to talk over your head, won't go away, and keeps asking for money.

Financial issues are very serious and important to people. But this approach was providing a more interesting and entertaining way for them to do it...that made them want to come in! What is the purpose of a seminar anyway? To get people to come in and see you, right? Well if you're going to get them to come and see you, first you have to get people to show up. Let's face it. Seminars must compete with other forms of entertainment for people's time and attention. Most seminars have marginal entertainment value.

Whether or not a seminar is entertaining depends on two factors: material (what you present) and delivery (how you present it). Delivery is critical of course. Some people are better at it than others. But no matter how good you are, it's hard to make dry technical content interesting enough to grab people's attention and motivate them to come in.

Not only is this form of seminar more interesting, because of the show and play and the Q&A, it also allows each seminar to be customized to the audience that you're working with. And it doesn't get old because of the range of options and different things you can illustrate.

But what was it about this approach that made it both entertaining *and* productive? I found this out by 'surprise.'

⭐ The Power of Positive Surprise

I met Dr. A. and his wife, Sue, at his office. Dan was a successful doctor in a small town. He was planning to retire in four years, at age 62. They owned a successful practice, a small farm, and had saved well. They lived comfortably and did not have an extravagant lifestyle.

I knew that they had already met with another advisor—someone who they had known for a very long time. If I was going to get their business, I was going to have to do more than show them another plain-vanilla 'simulated leather binder' printed plan. I was going to have to really differentiate myself.

After I gathered the data, I illustrated the results. There were no surprises. Given the assumptions we made, they were going to be fine—and they knew it. In a funny way I felt like I failed because I couldn't tell them anything they didn't already know. I definitely had not differentiated myself from the pack with what I had done...*yet.*

I shifted strategies and took another shot with a more playful scenario approach. "Would you like to see what it would look like if you retired today?" They joked with each other about what they would do as I made the change. They seemed surprised (and pleased) when they saw they could.

Then I took it a step further...I asked him, "Would you like to see what it would look like if you retired today and couldn't sell your practice?" It was like I let the air out of him. A big part of their current plan, at least in their minds, involved the ability to sell Dan's practice. I think that deep down, they both feared the possibility that either they couldn't sell it or wouldn't get enough, but they hadn't faced up to it. I made the change. The result surprised us all - it made a difference but was not as bad as they had expected. As it turned out, small changes to his retirement plan made a big difference—and most anything else he did would not. As we analyzed it, this made perfect sense, but they had never thought about it. Still, the result was not as good as the original scenario.

So now what? I had to make a decision regarding the next step. I could change the retirement age back, reduce their lifestyle, increase expected return rates, or...come up with more money. I asked, "What if we sell the farm?" Dan's response was strong and immediate. "No. We are NOT going to sell the farm." (Have you ever tried to get a farmer to sell a farm?) I looked over at Sue. She was sitting next to him with her hands folded with a look that pleaded, 'Please sell the farm.'

I decided to play it out. "Well, let's see what it would look like if you did." As I started to change it, Dan protested. The new graphic popped up. The sale had a dramatic effect. Their net worth soared. Both of them sat for a moment, trying to get their arms around what they were seeing. So, I summarized. "This scenario illustrates what would happen if: (a) you retired today; (b) you were not able to sell your practice, and (c) you sold the farm."

Dan asked, "It would make *that much* difference if we sold the farm?" After a brief pause he said, "Sell half the farm." Their situation still looked very good. He glanced briefly at Sue, then back to me and said, "Put in $100,000 expense for an airplane." Sue protested. Dan raised his voice and pounded on the table as he said, "If I'm going to sell half the farm, I'm going to get an airplane." I put the plane in. It still looked good—better than where we started. Dan said, "Retire me in two years—at 60." I adjusted the retirement age.

It was like the pieces of puzzle coming together. Dan looked at Sue, then me, and said excitedly, **"That's what I want!"** I shifted gears and explained a potential strategy for achieving this. They became clients.

As we wrapped up, I asked them, "Was this helpful for you today?" They answered enthusiastically, "Yes! We got exactly what we wanted. And it wasn't at all what we expected to see."

Reflections: As I left, I felt a real sense of accomplishment, and a new respect for the power of positive surprise.

We hear so many companies talking about the importance of *exceeding client expectations*…but that's usually all it is—talk. How do you actually do it?

Planning and selling that applies the concept of positive surprise provides us with a way to deliver it! For example:

- If somebody expects to retire in two years, see if they can do it in one year…or today!
- If somebody expects to spend $50,000 per year in retirement, show them if they can spend $60,000.
- Show them what's possible or what it will take to do better than they expect.

Using technology in front of people allowed me to take advantage of 'in-the-moment' opportunities: things they said or a look on one of their faces. It allowed me to stretch them and take them beyond where they expected. How else would I have been able to play out Sue's silent plea to sell the farm or Dan's desire for an airplane as compromise?

This is something that simply isn't possible with a paper-based planning approach! This is what differentiated me from other sales advisors and helped me earn their business.

Why Can't You Try on Financial Solutions Before You Buy Them?

Dr. David T. and his wife Jane faced a difficult decision (and a deadline). Six months ago the hospital offered to buy his business—both the practice and the building. It was a good offer. At age 60, he felt this was probably the right time to sell and retire. They received the offer six months earlier. They had two more weeks before it took place. Their attorney suggested they consider a Charitable Remainder Trust (CRT).

Dr. and Mrs. T. felt good, but not great, about their financial position. The $750,000 they would receive was about ½ of their net worth. Between this and their 401(k) they had approximately $1.4M. They felt this would be adequate to provide for the standard of living they had become accustomed to. But when their accountant explained the tax implications of the sale, they became concerned. The tax was going to be about $150,000.

"Over your lifetime, the money you save from not paying capital gains tax will compound... provide you income...and when you die, it will result in lower estate taxes."

Jane's eyes glazed over. It sounded very logical, but she couldn't get past the idea that they would be giving away almost half of their assets. Things hadn't always been this good. $600,000 after tax sounded good ...and tangible ...and safe. So who cared if the IRS got a little more money?

Dr. T. had a pretty good handle on the concept and mechanics of the trust. He did his research. He talked to others who had done it. In his mind, if he could save a substantial amount of money in taxes and still benefit from it personally, he was for it. But he wouldn't do it without Jane's buy in.

Their attorney brought me in to take a final last-ditch stab at the CRT presentation. As I gathered information, their case took shape on the wall in front of us. I presented the 'sell it and pay taxes' scenario first. Given their relatively conservative investment style, the outcome wasn't as good as they had hoped. To avoid dipping into principal in their mid-70's they would have to take a more aggressive investment approach, or accept a lower retirement income. Neither of them appeared pleased with these alternatives.

So, I made the changes necessary to illustrate the 'charitable' scenario. The graphic results were dramatically better—with the same income and investment assumptions. "How can we *give away* that much money and be better off?" asked Jane. When I pulled the two scenarios up side by side, the difference was clear. The charitable option provided more income and allowed them to take less from their retirement account. By taking less early the amount grew much faster. The result was that now they would not dip into their investment principal until their late '80s.

Jane said, "I never would have understood that unless I saw it. If it makes that much difference, let's do it." They were delighted. Six months of agonizing were over; their retirement dreams were achievable; her fears were addressed; the decision was made.

Reflections: Would you buy a car you've never test-driven or a house you've never walked through...because a salesperson performs a needs analysis and tells you they've found a good fit? For most people the answer is NO! Then why do we sell financial services this way?

You don't have to if you have tools and a sales method that let people 'try on' financial solutions before they buy them. By bringing the right equipment in the room and knowing how to use it with them, I was able to let people try on different possibilities and tailor the solutions that best 'suit' them.

I also recognized the power of using this visual interactive approach to collaborate with other sales advisors. When the attorney had questions or gave input, I was able to integrate it. This created a situation where all the minds (clients' and sales advisors') were in the room at the same time…and were able to feed off of each other's ideas and questions. It made the meeting feel like an open panel discussion that was beneficial and informative for all the parties involved.

Trust Doesn't Take Time, It Takes Risk

Greg, a financial advisor and good friend, asked me to join him for a meeting with Vince, one of his clients, who was a local business owner. Greg suggested that even though it was one of his current clients, this meeting would be worth my time since Vince was a bright guy who was well respected and influential in the community.

Vince had been a client of his for five years and although Greg had some of his investments, he was sure that Vince had other assets he hadn't told him about. Greg also told me that Vince was very protective of his information and unlikely to share much in a first meeting with me.

We started the interview process and Greg's assessment was accurate. Vince was friendly but cautious. He didn't hide the fact that he had other assets, but he played them down and suggested that we plan as if they didn't exist. I completed the interview process with the information that we knew and he was willing to share.

Next, I pulled up the graphs I typically show, starting with Net Worth. It was apparent that Vince wouldn't run out of assets, but as we looked at the graph of net worth and the value of his estate, you could tell something was bothering him.

Vince said, "I want you to add a rental property valued at $500,000. I plan to sell it in five years. Now what does it look like?" I made the change and we reviewed the results again with the new data. The net worth looked better. We moved on to a discussion of cash flow.

Because most of his wealth was in property and his business, Vince was highly illiquid. The analysis suggested he wouldn't have enough money to support his retirement unless he sold the business.

Then he told me, "I want you to add $1 million in cash. Let's see what it looks like now!"

The look on Greg's face spoke volumes. He suspected the $500,000 property. The $1 million… this was new territory. I added the cash and re-ran the illustrations. The changes were substantial. This was what he wanted to see.

I probed to learn more. "Tell me more about the additions, Vince. I want to make sure I'm giving you an accurate picture."

"They're properties I've owned for some time. One I just sold…the other I plan to sell within five years."

"How would you like me to illustrate what you do with the proceeds? Do you plan to buy more property? Leave it in cash? Or invest it?"

"I'll probably put half of it in another property. I'm considering investing the other half...What would you do with it if I gave it to you?"

Since he needed some income, I illustrated a balanced portfolio designed to give him the income he needed and some growth.

"I have some additional income coming in from the other property. So, I'm not as concerned about income right now." (More new information.)

Then I turned to Greg and asked, "What do you suggest in terms of a growth portfolio?" As Greg and Vince talked, I made the adjustments. Then I pulled up the illustrations with the changes suggested.

This illustration looked like what Vince wanted to see. The strategy and illustration struck a chord with him. "I like your suggestions about how you'd do that...I think that's what I want to do."

We shifted into a discussion about next steps. Before the meeting concluded, Vince was setting up another appointment with us to bring in a check.

After the meeting, Greg told me that Vince opened up and shared more information in this one meeting, than he had in all the time he had spent with him up to date. He learned about new assets and goals...he was able to discuss strategy, illustrate solutions, and move towards implementation...and opened a new account with a current client as a result.

Reflections: This story and others like it have led us to challenge one of the financial service industry pillars of conventional wisdom—that 'trust takes time.' No it doesn't! In case after case, we find people leaking information that they've never told us or anyone else for that matter, often the first time we talked with them. Greg had Vince as a client for five years. Vince was a very cautious and private guy. What caused him to 'go deep' and share information with me: someone he had just met?

To understand this better, I asked Dr. David Lazenby to explain trust from a psychologist's perspective. The answer is as powerful as it is profound. He said:

"Are you talking about the noun or the verb? The noun, trust, means comfort. The verb, trust, means taking risk. People commonly confuse these because they don't know the difference.

It's not that time and trust aren't related. There are lots of good examples where they go hand in hand. But trust doesn't require time. Trust requires risk. When you ask someone to trust you, you're not asking them to feel comfortable. You're asking them to make themselves vulnerable.

The feeling of trust comes from making yourself vulnerable and getting validated rather than violated. That's why trust requires creating an environment that validates people and rewards them for taking risk. If you create a *validating environment*, people will 'trust' you long before they have the feeling of trust."

Building trust faster! As I look back on it, and other examples like this, I now understood how this could happen. In a paper-based planning world, there was only the potential for delayed reward…days or weeks later. Without a more immediate incentive to take risks, what drives the decision to share information? Comfort! Vince may not have felt comfortable with me yet, but there was an immediate reward for disclosing additional information. I was getting information because I was providing an environment that rewarded him for disclosing information and taking risks right now.

Real Life Isn't Simple…It's Complex!

I was working with Ed, an entrepreneur who had recently sold his business for approximately $7 million dollars. He was in his early 70's, widowed, and very frugal. He knew he couldn't spend it all, and he was very interested in having influence over his legacy.

Ed was very concerned about leaving "too much" to his children. He believed that, "If you don't earn it, you don't appreciate it." He decided that he wanted to leave enough to his children and grandchildren to provide them supplemental income, but he didn't want to make them rich. He was also very involved in his church and local social organizations. He was looking for a way to help others and give something back.

A case like this seems like a financial advisor's dream. There are so many things you can do. But the real challenge is to make *something* happen. Ed had been working with a couple of other sales advisors and had several plans he hadn't implemented. What was wrong? He had goals. He had resources. He had good sales advisors. He wasn't an indecisive person. What was holding him up? He could see the parts, but he was having a hard time getting his arms around 'the big picture.' Every time he made a change in one plan, it had direct impact on the others that he wanted to reconsider. He had been at this for months and felt like he was going around in circles.

He was trying to make decisions about his *wealth*. This involved investment plans, charitable gifting, family gifting, inheritance, taxes, and of course planning for his retirement income and security. As I listened to his interests and concerns, I drew them out on a white board and 'the big picture' began to take shape. The decisions he was faced with were organized around six boxes involving:

- Who would benefit from his wealth?
- When they would get it?

Who Benefits?	When	
	DURING LIFE	**AT DEATH**
Self & Spouse	① Lifestyle Issues	② First Death Issues
Heirs & Others	③ Family Gifting	④ Inheritance
Charity & IRS	⑤ Social Gifting	⑥ Social Legacy

Once we laid it out this way, it was easier for us to talk about individual changes, because we could **see** how each decision affected each of the other parties. The big picture provided a meaningful container for the pieces.

None of the other sales advisors were capable of showing the ripple effect on each of these decisions—the tradeoffs between retirement, charitable, and family decisions. That's why every time he previously had a question, it was back to the drawing board. We were able to model this for him and help him visualize the tradeoffs between the competing goals and objectives of the various plans he was considering. He got the answers he was looking for. And as a result, we were able to manage his entire estate, which resulted in over $5 million in investments under management.

Reflections: I began to understand and define wealth management as a systems (big picture) problem. From an advisor's perspective the client's financial life may look like parts: retirement planning; investment planning; estate planning and others. But from the consumer's perspective, wealth management is one big whole. It describes all the things that can happen to their money. Decisions in one part affect the others. When you divide this financial big picture into pieces, it may be simpler to perform calculations, but you will create roadblocks to customer's decisions unless you can show how changes to the parts affect the big picture.

We got this account because we were able to explain how to address the complex problem this client faced and show him what the big picture looked like.

When I asked Dr. Lazenby about this, he told me, "To researchers, the problem you were dealing with is commonly called 'the bubble hypothesis.' Picture putting a sticker on a car window...you usually have air bubbles underneath it, don't you? As you press down on one part of the sticker to push an air bubble out, you often create new bubbles. The trick is to anticipate this occurring, so you don't just keep moving the bubble. This usually requires smoothing out the whole sticker; not simply pressing down on each bubble that pops up."

This gave me a new way to describe the way that sales advisors create value for clients. People don't need sales advisors to help them solve simple problems and in the Internet Age, there are many other places clients can go to get information. The *real* value sales advisors provide today comes from helping people understand and manage the tradeoffs involved in the *complex* decisions they face.

The more complex a problem is:

- The more difficult it is to make a decision unless the client can understand the system (see the big picture) and balance (visualize) the tradeoffs involved
- The greater the need for a true scenario planning process to consider multiple alternatives
- And the greater the need for simulation tools to illustrate the impact of decisions—their ripple effect on other issues.

But...Where Do You Find Tools to Do This?

I tried looking for tools that would help me: look at the big picture, run multiple scenarios, and play out simulations...with the customer! Where could I find a tool to work like a... decision flight simulator?

After looking at hundreds of software programs, I realized that not only weren't there any programs specifically designed for this, but that most available programs actually make it harder to solve complex problems because they're:

(A) *Modular*—they separate the issues and look at the parts not the whole

(B) *Print-based*—they're designed primarily for making printouts

(C) *Backroom Tools*—they're designed to be used away from the customer, not in front of them

The characteristics may be effective to print out traditional planning 'books', projections, and sales illustrations, but they are severely limited in helping sales advisors and clients simulate decisions and play out scenarios. That's because they're simply not designed to do this.

Imagine taking the current software you use, projecting it on the wall, and asking your age 55+ clients to try and read it from 15-20 feet away for a seminar (or 5 feet away in a conference room for that matter). Forget it. I began to recognize the need for a new program—one that looked like presentation software but worked like analytical software.

I looked at every program available in the industry. The problem was that they all looked like newspapers. I was looking for television. The analytical tools were hard to look at (and impossible to show someone). The presentation tools were dumbed down. I wanted a program with beauty and brains...

And you also may have noticed that in none of the cases here, except the first one, did I have a printed plan prepared ahead of time. It became more apparent as I worked on these cases that people didn't need the printouts to make decisions. They only used them to validate decisions they had already made. They were making decisions as a result of playing out visual scenarios.

Where was I supposed to find a tool designed for comprehensive planning that wasn't designed for 'printing books' but for visually playing out scenarios and simulating results? I considered developing one, but wasn't sure I was willing to pay the cost or extend the effort to do it.

The next case helped me make up my mind.

Together or Apart? Building a Shared Vision

Bill and Diane, ages 65/62, were at a crossroads. After 30 years of marriage, raising 3 kids, and successfully growing a business, they were preparing for retirement. It should have been a happy story, but it wasn't. They attended a seminar I gave and set up a meeting for me to review their financial situation as a result. I met them at their attorney's office. It was our first meeting.

Before I went in the room, the attorney pulled me aside. "Don't go in there yet. They're fighting." When I asked for information, he told me that their relationship had become increasingly strained and that they were actually considering divorce. When I entered the room, you could feel the icicles. They sat on the same side of the table—two chairs apart. I started the interview by asking for some basic information. Bill ran the show. Diane was silent.

Bill's Story. Bill was a successful real estate developer. He owned both commercial and residential properties worth about $4 million dollars. In addition, he and Diane had about $1 million in investments. They had become accustomed to an upscale lifestyle of approximately $200k per year. According to Bill, here's what retirement looked like: No major changes to their current situation; he would continue to work part time managing the properties; their lifestyle would go unchanged.

I entered the data while we talked. We completed all of the questions to create a basic financial plan in about 20 minutes. The graphic results projected on the wall were very clear. The strategy as he described it would work. Bill looked at Diane as if to say, "See! I told you." During this entire time, Diane had said nothing, just sitting with her arms crossed. I shifted my attention to her. "What would you do differently?" I asked. For the next 15 minutes, she unloaded her view of retirement...while Bill sat silently with his arms crossed.

Diane's Story. In her mind, Bill's plan may have been logical but made no sense. She knew what he looked like when he got up in the morning. "He can't continue to stay on top of the properties 'part time.'" Diane was a real estate salesperson. She wanted to sell the properties, take the money, put it in the market, and live off the investment. They had worked hard, now it was time to cash out and reap the rewards. When I modeled her vision of retirement, the results also looked very good. And then it hit me…

Without saying anything, I pulled the two plans up side-by-side. The graphs told a fascinating story. Despite completely opposite approaches to the problem, the difference in projected net worth 30 years later was relatively small. They sat there stunned. After a few minutes of silence, Bill turned to Diane and said, "If that's the only difference between them, I'll do it your way." The ice had broken.

Results. When they left, Bill shook my hand all the way from the conference room to the front door. When I called the attorney the next day he said, "What did you do to them? They're talking again!" The end result for me was a multi-million dollar investment client. The end result for them was a mutual understanding of where they stood, what they could have, and a shared vision of what they wanted. Neither "won." They created a new reality together.

After the appointment, I called Dr. Lazenby looking for a professional's insight into what took place. If I did something right I wanted to be able to repeat it. He mentioned that people tend to generalize off of their own experience—because it happened to them, it's real. "I'm right and if you're different you must be wrong." Like a scientist with an 'n-sample' of 1, their views are usually never challenged or validated, but they become the basis for strongly held beliefs. And this makes it very difficult for people to think about or talk about highly emotional issues.

Reflections: When you have people with differing views on a subject and want to help them build a shared vision, you can help by providing a way for them to *see their thinking* and *talk about it*. It would have been impossible to try to talk them through this. Attempts made to talk it out usually resulted in win/lose discussions. Words aren't enough to overcome long-time deeply held impressions.

A visual collaborative approach provided a more effective way for them to understand their options; to see the value and challenges in each other's solutions; to build dreams and to take action—together.

This case, about the couple considering divorce, was the case that pushed me over the edge personally and professionally. I had a new perspective of what I did for a living and a new respect for the power of using technology to facilitate collaborative learning and decision-making. This wasn't about selling or creating a plan. It was about changing people's lives.

It's been several years since this meeting and I still get choked up every time I tell this story. I recognized that I had found a new and very powerful way to really help people that worked faster and had better results than a 'traditional' planning/sales approach. This was something I wanted to share with other sales advisors. But I still wasn't sure how to explain what 'it' was.

It All Added Up!

As I reflected back on these experiences…it all started to add up. I wasn't using the laptop and projector in old traditional ways. I was using technology to:

- Enable recovery from mistakes and wrong assumptions
- Get more and better information…to improve the interview process
- Shorten the sales cycle by eliminating unnecessary delays and meetings
- Change the sales process from a series of boring and painful meetings to an engaging and interesting session of interactive financial play
- Utilize the power of positive surprise as a way to deliver on the promise of exceeding customer expectations and helping capture and keep people's attention
- Help people play out dreams and fears and create new goals
- Let people try on solutions before they have to live them or buy them
- Develop trust faster
- Help people solve complex problems with a big picture approach
- Facilitate collaboration to get people on the same page; to help them work and make decisions together
- Sell WITH people instead of selling TO them

Visual…Interactive…Planning…and Selling…VIPS! With tools designed to simulate decisions and play out scenarios. Blending high-tech and high-touch for *fast professional selling*.

Each story helped me understand how to improve the experience and results of the financial planning process for clients and sales advisors through the appropriate use of technology!

But how would I train someone else to do it? When I tried teaching others, I realized that:

- A baseline set of skills in planning, selling, and using technology was required.
- I couldn't find any current tools or training designed to support VIP selling.
- I was promoting an approach that flew directly in the face of the conventional sales wisdom and established methods of the financial services industry.
- To sell collaboratively with customers, new tools, new methods, and new skills were required.

I was faced with a difficult decision. Let it go or go for it. The impact this approach has had on people's lives and in sales results was so compelling, I knew I couldn't let it go. But I needed additional expertise—especially in the area of how people can utilize technology to improve decision making. I found an expert in these subjects and we began the process of researching and writing this book.

Conclusion—The ScenarioSelling Story

The story of ScenarioSelling is the story of what Dr. David Lazenby and I have learned and what we've accomplished as we've developed a system for sales professionals to solve problems and sell more effectively with visual interactive technology.

Our company, ScenarioNow Inc., develops the training and tools to facilitate the type of interaction and results you read about here. The stories here are only an introduction. During the last 7 years, we have completed the most comprehensive research on applying technology to professional selling ever attempted.

Today, thousands of sales advisors across the country including CPAs, trust officers, attorneys, insurance agents, securities representatives, and others are using our tools to plan this way by...

- Blending high-tech and high-touch...
- Visual...Interactive...Planning...and Selling...
- Technology-based collaboration for fast professional selling...

This approach makes it much easier to find out their prospects' real needs and illustrate the value of your solutions. And it provides dramatic improvements in sales productivity. *And most importantly clients prefer it.*

But despite the advantages, we know that there are many sales advisors and companies who either can't or won't be able to do this...for three primary reasons: they haven't had the right tools to do it (what they use); it requires new skills and different methods (how they use the tools); and it goes against many of the 'rules' of the current paradigm for professional selling (why they do it this way).

We've developed the *theory, methods,* and *tools* that will make technology-based collaborative selling the new paradigm and standard for professional selling. We provide software and training to help people sell visually and interactively. Our scientifically valid state-of-the-art system helps people develop the skills necessary to make the transition easier and faster.

Parts II, III, and IV of this book give a formal structure to the discoveries in Part I—the what, the why, and the how of the ScenarioSelling system.

If you're interested and would like to learn more, contact us, or visit our website, www.scenarioselling.com for additional information and recently written articles.

We look forward to hearing from you and learning how we can help you create your own scenario success stories.

SELLING —
PAST & PRESENT

Part II

Part II
Part II
Part II

INTRODUCTION

"Teachers open the door, but you must enter by yourself."
—Chinese Proverb

In Part I of this book, we provided the background—the stories and experiences that lead us to develop ScenarioSelling.

Parts II, III, and IV make up the 'formal' book. They describe the what, why, and how of the ScenarioSelling process.

We start out in Part II with *Selling Past & Present*: a description of the current state of selling and its relationship to technology to help illustrate the problem our system is designed to solve.

DEATH OF THE SALESMAN?

"The purpose of marketing is to make selling superfluous."
—Peter Drucker

During the last 100 years, there have been more changes and improvements in the way people work and live than in all of human history. Technologies like the production line, the transistor, the television, the laser, the computer, and the Internet have advanced and changed the way companies produce, promote, and service goods. And they've dramatically changed what consumers have, what they want, what they expect, and how they get it.

But in the last 100 years there have been relatively few advances in sales process (the way people sell). Of course, there have been advances in selling, but mostly in the development of sales tools, which have either supported existing low-tech sales practices and processes, or are designed to remove sales middlemen from the buying process. This, in turn, has created and continues to foster the perception that selling must either be *high-touch* (people & no technology) or *high-tech* (technology & no people).

Does professional selling have a place in the emerging digital marketplace? Or are salespeople destined to be the milkmen of the 21st century—intermediaries whose jobs have been replaced by new forms of technology-enabled promotion and distribution?

This book will illustrate the following points:

- Technology changes, consumer changes, and market forces are causing professional selling to undergo its first major transition since the Eisenhower era.
- Some types of selling and salespeople will be left behind.

- Technology will replace salespeople for many but not all types of selling.
- Selling isn't high-tech or high-touch. Technology is an inseparable part of selling. The problem isn't technology; it's what we do with it.
- The perception that high-tech selling and high-touch selling are incompatible is caused by the lack of integration between sales tools and the sales process.
- Integrating new Digital Age tools into the sales process will fundamentally and irrevocably change the way people sell.
- The end result will dramatically improve sales productivity, the customer's sales experience, and the image of the sales professional.

To understand what these changes are and what the 'new selling' will look like, let's start by looking at the impact of technology on buying.

21st Century Buyer

Digital technologies like the personal computer and the Internet have advanced and changed the way companies market, sell, and service goods. And they've dramatically changed what consumers expect, what they buy, and how they get it.

The changes in those sales and information-gathering tools have changed consumers themselves.

Consumers expect more...better...cheaper

Consumers no longer need a friend in the business (or a salesperson) to get inside information. The growth of the information delivery industry lets consumers educate themselves about products and services 24 hours a day, seven days a week. They compare prices and performance ratings. They trade tips on how to bargain shop. They may know the exact wholesale price of an item, and expect to pay little more for it.

Search engines, like Pricegrabber.com scan the web like a personal shopper to help you filter through thousands of choices to find the best place and price to get what you want.

Faster...

Internet Age consumers are less tolerant of delays. A recent study showed that people don't even want to take the time to use a rotary-dial phone any more; they're accustomed to the quicker method of pushing a button. Website sellers like Amazon.com provide 'one-click' buying and overnight delivery of a wide variety of products and services.

And Friendlier!

As if those changes weren't enough, consumers want the buying process to be friendlier! Buying is no longer just a hunt-and-gather search for necessities for the modern consumer. It's an event. It's an experience. A company's sales efforts must compete for the consumer's attention with other forms of entertainment.

Many companies have figured out how to offer quality, service, and low cost, but fall down on the experience. Businesses that 'get it' (like REI and Bass Pro Shops with a mix of high-end sporting goods, waterfalls and climbing walls) are the ones expanding. At Build-A-Bear Workshop, you can create and build a teddy bear in a Pinocchio workshop—a better experience than simply buying one off the shelf. Barnes & Noble blends books, beverages and plush seating for an upscale café-book experience. Adults weaned on Chuck E. Cheese's pizza, games, and singing animals now have Dave & Buster's, a restaurant and lounge, where you can eat, drink, and play 18 holes of simulated golf (using clubs, not joysticks) or race motorcycles (the sit-on kind). It's hard to tell where the food ends and the entertainment begins.

Salespeople...Elimination?

If consumers can buy more, faster, easier, and better without them...then why do we need salespeople at all? Why not just eliminate the middleman completely?

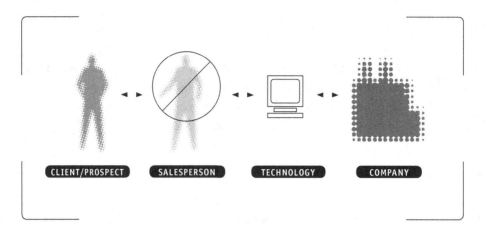

CLIENT/PROSPECT   SALESPERSON   TECHNOLOGY   COMPANY

Companies and salespeople have had several traditional answers for the continued existence of salespeople. Two of the most popular are the *'types of products'* and the *'types of people'* arguments.

- **Types of Products?** This suggests salespeople are needed for certain types of products: for example, luxury products and intangible goods or services.
- **Types of People?** This explanation suggests salespeople are needed for certain types of people: that some customers prefer 'self-help' and some simply prefer to buy from other people.

But, during the last 10 years we've seen *more people* are buying *more products* without salespeople in the process. So, while both of these explanations have some surface validity, they provide a relatively shallow and weak foundation to base the future of the sales profession on. Salespeople are increasingly being replaced by technological innovations that make it easier for customers to go directly to companies.

Can Technology Eliminate the Need for Salespeople? We've seen many examples of how technology has changed the way that people buy. Modern advances like ATM's, kiosks, and the Internet have allowed consumers to get buying 'self-help.' Many of the things salespeople have traditionally done to create value for the customer can be replaced by technology.

It seems reasonable to assume that advances in technology will expand and improve our ability to help ourselves and as a result continue to take salespeople out of the process. Companies continue to condition consumers to expect more information, more access, and less human contact. Will marketing, selling, and information technologies eliminate the need for salespeople? Many experts think so.

But television didn't eliminate radio, home videos didn't eliminate the Cineplex, and tax-preparation software didn't lead to the extinction of accountants. People still want music and news without pictures. They still want the experience of seeing a movie on the big screen. And they still want a human's advice when making difficult decisions.

Technological innovations don't necessarily eliminate tasks and jobs. They do change how they're done, and how they're valued, however. Technology won't eliminate selling, but it will change how people sell and how they create value for customers. It will force selling and salespeople to evolve—to change their processes and the way they use technology.

⭐ Or Evolution?

Why must professional selling change with advances in technology? Simple. Because of the relationship between technology, value creation, and selling.

(1) *Technological advances change the way value is created.* When intermediaries (middlemen) are involved in a process, like production, marketing, distribution, or selling, advances in technology disrupt and change what they do. Companies that lag behind the technology curve risk disintermediation (being taken out of the middle).

(2) *Salespeople will only be included in the customer buying process if they continue to provide value.*

(3) *Since the way they create value for customers is changing, salespeople must adapt and find new ways to create value or suffer the consequences.*

The position of salespeople who won't or can't find new ways to provide value will be eliminated. Like Willie Loman in Arthur Miller's classic play "Death of a Salesman," they will find themselves increasingly marginalized as the world changes and they do not. Unless they evolve, these sales dinosaurs will be bringing about their own demise.

⭐ Moving Forward

Salespeople and companies who adapt will do better than survive; they will thrive. The new world will be better for consumers, companies and salespeople. Salespeople and companies will work more efficiently and reap higher profits. Consumers will get the goods and services they want, faster and more effectively.

Are we ready? Usage indicates that consumers are increasingly comfortable with information technologies. Are salespeople equally prepared? It's now accepted that most salespeople need computers. Just giving salespeople computers doesn't mean their sales methods will make the changes we believe are necessary to compete effectively in the new economic era we have entered.

So what changes are required and what will the new landscape look like? A recent commercial parodied the investment sales business with a broker saying, "Let's put some lipstick on this pig." Selling in the 21st century needs more than just a technological makeover. A new sales discipline, including new skills, attitudes, tools, and methods, designed with technology in mind, is needed.

To see where we're going, let's start by looking at where we've been. The next chapter provides a "History of Selling" that parallels the impact of technology on 20th century production, marketing, and selling. Understanding the role of technology in selling's history will illustrate why evolution is inevitable. It also points out what changes are necessary and what results are likely.

THE MODERN HISTORY OF SELLING

"Those who don't understand history are doomed to repeat its mistakes."
—George Santayana

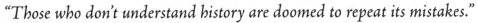

Selling—Not a Textbook Case

Sales as a formal field of study gets every bit the respect Rodney Dangerfield used to claim in his nightclub act.

While most business schools typically award degrees for those who study marketing, production, and management; there are few bachelors programs with degrees for sales study; and almost none with post-graduate studies. Most academic professionals treat selling as alchemy rather than science…a chapter in a marketing text to be skipped if you need to make up time.

So where do salespeople get the knowledge and skills required? Ask almost any salesperson and they'll tell you—on the job.

Professions Have Histories

Other respected professions have histories that are passed on as part of their training programs. American attorneys learn how our legal system developed from the British model. American doctors trace their history as a respected, separate profession to the 19th-century formation of the American Medical Society, and place their roots even farther back in the Middle East and Ancient Greece.

Teaching and counseling are more recent examples of professions that earned greater respect as more formal histories of the fields were developed and the science behind them became more clearly established. Before the first counselor education programs, in the mid-1950's, counselors passed on their skills by mentoring. They've since developed a scientific (theory-methods-tools) approach that has dramatically enhanced their professional standing.

Other business disciplines like production and marketing illustrate histories that help us understand the science and the models behind them. But where is the history of selling?

The History of Selling?

Selling has no authoritative history. Why not? One of the problems is that selling is one of the world's oldest professions. Some of the oldest clay tablets found in the Middle East are bills of sale. There's even a joke that credits a celestial salesman for persuading God that creation was a good idea. While that story belongs to the vast body of amusing sales apocrypha, it is certain that even when early societies relied on barter as a medium of exchange, sales skills were important. It's easy to imagine that one farmer or another always got more goats in exchange for his barley beer because he knew how to talk up the quality of his brew.

Selling's oral tradition is a likely reason there are so few formal studies of sales. Because selling doesn't have a 'legitimate' written history, it suffers from having many illegitimate anecdotal versions. In fact, many people claim to be the 'father' of selling passing on their knowledge by telling stories of their triumphs, instead of scientifically challenging and validating their theories, methods, and tools.

This lack of a formal history is one of the key factors that handicaps attempts to legitimize the selling profession. Without a history, there's no 'science'; without science there's no validity; without validity, no respect.

We believe that establishing a formal history for selling will improve its standing as a profession, but even more importantly provide a model to understand its past and its future. But where...or when... should we begin?

A Shared History Model

We chose to approach this problem by constructing a shared history model that parallels selling's relationship with production and marketing—for two reasons:

- Production and marketing are relatively recent (20th century) disciplines. Their pedigrees are traceable.
- There are strong parallels in how all three (production, marketing, and selling) have changed with advances in technology.

The benefit of this approach is that we get more than just a picture of where selling has been; it gives us clues about where selling is going.

Our model divides the 20th century into three ages: The Machine Age, The Information Age, and The Digital Age—three periods that we suggest comprise the modern history of selling.

	The Modern History of Selling		
	Machine Age	**Information Age**	**Digital Age**
Defining Technologies	Assembly Line	Transistor; Television	Integrated Circuit; Computers
Production Methods	Mass Production	Batch Production	Mass Customization
Marketing Methods	Mass Marketing	Target Marketing	One to One Marketing
Selling Methods	Transactional Selling	Consultative Selling	??? Selling

The transition from one Age to the next was sparked by the introduction of a new paradigm shifting technology and the innovations that resulted from it. Each of these major technological advances changed how value was created for customers, subsequently changing the Production, Marketing, and Sales methods required.

It also is important to acknowledge that each of these ages laid the foundation for the next, because without the knowledge and infrastructure each provided, the next age wouldn't be possible: without dinosaurs, no birds. Despite the advances of each new age, prior methods of production, marketing, and selling still cling to life although their influence and ability to create value fades. That's why we can still see evidence of each era today, just as crocodiles have continued to exist even though they are no longer the last word in life forms.

When we look at the patterns in selling's shared history and we consider the relatively recent (last 20 years) and dramatic impact of digital technologies on production and marketing, the implications are clear. A new way of creating value has arrived; Selling is undergoing its first major change since the Eisenhower Era; and salespeople must adapt their sales methods or be banished to the swampy, fetid outskirts of the marketplace.

To help set the stage for our modern history story, let's take a brief look at selling's pre-history.

Pre-History—The Artisan Age

Large-scale production and marketing didn't come into their own until the 20th century. For the purpose of our model, we refer to the time before this (selling's pre-history) as the Artisan Age.

In the Artisan Age, craftsmen made products individually, by hand. Everything was 'custom made.' The value of the products was based on the individual craftsman's skill. Sales were made either by the craftsman who created the object, or by local merchants, with traveling salespeople, or peddlers, sometimes taking part in the mercantile process.

Transition #1—From the Artisan Age to the Machine Age

The Industrial Revolution of the late 19th and early 20th centuries brought the end of the Artisan Age and the beginning of the modern history of selling. Eli Whitney, the same inventor who brought us the cotton gin and perhaps by extension the American Civil War, modified crafts production methods and introduced the first modern production model—the American System of Manufactures. This system used standardized parts, but had each craftsman assemble his product from beginning to end. [2.1] The craftsmen moved from workstation to workstation as their products evolved. (*The people moved…the product sat still.*)

In a nice bit of industrial symmetry (and historical irony), Whitney's system was used to develop guns for the Union Army and help bring about an end to the Civil War. It also laid the foundation for the next step in the evolution of technology, the mobile assembly line, which gave birth to the Machine Age.

The Machine Age

Starting in the early 1900s and all the way to the 1950s, the Machine Age reigned supreme.

	Machine Age
Timeframe	1900-1950's
Defining Technology	Assembly Line
Scarce Resources	Capital
Value Created By	Economies of Scale; Access to Capital
Scale	Large
Competition / Choice	None
Production Method	Mass Production
Marketing Method	Mass Marketing
Selling Method	Transactional

Mass Production

Henry Ford's 1913 mobile assembly line introduced the world's first true *mass production* system. In addition to new tools and equipment, it introduced a critical change in production process design. Before the mobile assembly line, it was the people that moved from bench to bench to work on stationary products. The assembly line reversed it. Now the people sat still and the products moved!

Cars could now be built in hours instead of days. Identical consumer goods rolled past workers whose hands made identical motions to tighten identical bolts hour after hour, day after day.

Henry Ford's introduction of the assembly line changed more than just the way products were made. It changed the way that businesses were structured and the way they created value. Companies gathered the capital required for the huge factories needed to provide economies of scale.

The object was to make and sell as many of them as possible. Only by selling a great number of his identical manufactured goods could a company owner hope to recoup the enormous costs of setting up a factory and hiring a work force.

As more cars were sold, prices dropped because it cost less per unit to make each Model T. As prices came down, more people could afford the vehicles, and even more were sold.

They were able to take advantage of the resulting efficiencies to dominate their market places. By 1928, Model T's sold for $290. General Motors, Chrysler, and Ford controlled 80 percent of the automobile market. Hundreds of now-forgotten automobile makers were left in the 'Big Three's' rear-view mirror.

Mass Marketing

Marketing in the machine age was typified by Henry Ford's classic comment, "The customer can have any color he wants, as long as he wants black." Consumers were seen as the passive recipients of whatever manufactured largesse captains of industry chose to offer.

The multitudes, thrilled to have an item once reserved for the rich, happily bought the now affordable, mass-produced automobiles, regardless of the limited choice in colors. The triumph of Ford and the black Model T is one of the purest examples of the strengths of this age. Ford had sufficient capital to build a large manufacturing plant, and the vision to innovate efficient production methods. Millions of his cars rolled off the assembly lines. Dealerships popped up in towns, large and small, all over the country.

The growth of commercial radio in the 1920's created an explosion in radio advertising. Soap powder producers sponsored daytime dramas. Ovaltine brought children the adventures of "Little Orphan Annie." Radio allowed advertisers to sing the virtues of their products from sea to shining sea. Consumers were buried with 'exposures' to new products paid for by program sponsors.

Transactional Selling

The growing consumer class swarmed into stores and onto car lots. And once there, the salesperson's job was not to find the best car for the person—indeed, the best car was whatever was on the lot! If you went to a Ford dealer, you got a Model T. "It's a great car...the best available," salesmen assured the consumers. And what a price!

Selling in the Machine Age was *transactional*. The role of the salesperson was 'pitchman'. The sales model for transactional selling is AIDA. [2.2]

+ Get Attention
+ Determine Interest
+ Demonstrate Features
+ Solicit Action

The delivery is the classic (and dreaded) 'sales pitch'. Consider the unwary grocery shopper. He ambles down the aisle, list in hand, and is confronted by a cheerful sausage demonstrator. "Hi, do you have a second? You like sausage don't you?" the demonstrator asks. Our consumer nods. "Here, try this. It's all-natural and smoked right here," the demonstrator states. Our consumer munches the sausage. "If you'd like to take it home today, here's a coupon," says the sausage seller. Our shopper strolls on, coupon in hand and perhaps a package of sausage as well. The entire sales process has taken just minutes.

With transactional selling, it doesn't matter if it's sausage or Chevrolets—it's the same methodology. You can almost hear the classic used car salesman promoting his product. "Look at this beauty. Do you want to get in and go for a drive? Somebody was just in here looking at it, so it may not be here tomorrow. Why don't we go in, and write this up today?"

This method is still used in many sales situations today and is responsible for the picture most people have of selling and salespeople.

Transition #2—From the Machine Age to the Information Age

The Machine Age's long decline began in 1947 when three Bell Labs scientists developed the transistor. The transition wasn't as dramatic as the comet streaking across the sky that brought about the end of the Dinosaur Age, but it was just as effective. The Information Age was at hand.

It was the age of *information arbitrage*. Access and control over information became as valuable, and then more valuable, than capital. This changed the rules for profitable competition in business.

The Information Age

	Machine Age	Information Age
Timeframe	1900-1950's	1940's-1990's
Defining Technology	Assembly Line	Transistor; Television
Scarce Resources	Capital	Information
Value Created By	Economies of Scale; Access to Capital	Information Arbitrage; Access to Information
Scale	Large	Smaller
Competition/Choice	None	Few
Production Method	Mass Production	Batch Production (EOQ)
Marketing Method	Mass Marketing	Target Marketing
Selling Method	Transactional	Consultative

Batch Production

Competition and choice increased significantly. Almost everyone who wanted a car already had one. The trick was to make consumers want newer and better ones—as often as possible. The genius of Henry Ford gave way to the genius of men like General Motors design-chief Harley Earl. If consumers wanted cars in colors other than black, in a new design every year, Earl and his team of designers would provide them.

Gathering and analyzing information about customer desires, in advance, became the key to efficiently producing batches in EOQ— Economically Optimal Quantities. [2.3] Production scale got smaller.

Manufacturing and retail businesses provide us great examples. Why have thousands of widgets sitting around in June when they wouldn't be needed until November? Inventory is expensive, after all. Why not make them around a plan, so we have just enough to meet demand?

Target Marketing

Transistors did for television what the production line did for cars (increased availability and reduced cost), changing TVs from a toy for the rich to an essential for the masses. In 1945, there were probably fewer than 10,000 television sets in the United States. News of World War II's end was carried by radio and newspaper. When American soldiers were sent to Korea in 1950, their countrymen saw the news on more than 6 million television sets. By the time John F. Kennedy debated Richard Nixon in 1960, there were almost 60 million sets for voters to watch from.

This critical mass gave birth to modern marketing and advertising. Marketing professionals began to segment the market and target their advertising messages to get the attention of groups of consumers thought most likely to buy them. They gathered information about the television and radio shows favored by different groups of listeners. Teens, listening to their ubiquitous transistor radios, and their families, gathered around the campfire of their televisions.

Consultative Selling

Transactional selling's effectiveness began to fade for many types of products as competition, choice, and information proliferated. Willy Loman's 'smile and a shoeshine' were no longer enough. He could no longer walk into a store with his sample case and expect the buyer to purchase just because Loman was well liked.

Buyers wanted their sellers to understand their needs and help them evaluate their options. Advances in information technology required more than just a change in the pitchman's delivery. It required a change in image and in process. To sell 'professionally' a new model was required.

Image. The image of the transactional salesperson as pitchman is a caricature in American culture. Consultative Selling was created as an attempt to professionalize selling. Consultative selling softens the whole assault on the senses, the pressure to do something and buy something in response to a bullet-proof (slick) sales presentation.

Process. Consultative selling is often referred to as 'needs based selling.' In it, the salesperson takes the prospect/client through an interview to determine whether a product or service is needed before the demonstration step begins.

The Consultative Model. A consultative selling model typically includes 5 sales *steps*:
- Building Rapport (Trust)
- Identifying Needs
- Demonstrating Solutions
- Overcoming Objections
- Closing the Sale

As a result of these process changes, consultative selling shifted the role and the image of the salesperson from a biased *pitchman* to an objective *consultant/expert*, who would help customers analyze their needs and choose the product or service that would best fit them.

For the last 40 years, consultative selling steps and the 'salesperson as consultant/expert' model have been the dominant paradigm for professional selling. Today, almost all professional selling programs are simply rehashed versions of the same material, spun around the latest sales guru's stories, and built on the same consultative sales process chassis.

Transition #3—From the Information Age to the Digital Age

"You have freedom of choice, but not freedom from choice."—Wendell Jones

The Information Age itself, like so many revolutions, carried the seeds of its own destruction. When information was scarce, it had great value. But as information became cheaper and easier to obtain, it began to flood the marketplace. Producers and consumers alike began to drown in it.

Decision-making became more complex as options began to overload people's attention capacity. Choosing any kind of consumer product or service began to take on the characteristics of a major research project. "Just give me a car, a phone, a television. Don't make me think about it," consumers began to whine, their collective heads buried in the symbolic sand.

Consumers and companies needed more effective ways to filter through the information and make it useful. Increasingly available and powerful tools for managing information, including computers and database software promised to make it possible.

The Information Age began to give way to the Digital Age.

The Digital Age

"Time is really the only capital that any human being has and the thing that he can least afford to waste or lose."—Thomas Edison

The Digital Age tells a story of tremendous changes in size, costs, power, and *speed*, that is once again rewriting the rules for profitable competition in business.

	Machine Age	Information Age	Digital Age
Timeframe	1900-1950's	1940's-1990's	1980's-Present
Defining Technologies	Assembly Line	Transistor; Television	Integrated Circuit; Computers
Scarce Resources	Capital	Information	Time & Attention
Value Created By	Economies of Scale; Access to Capital	Information Arbitrage; Access to Information	Fast Cycle Time; Reducing Complexity; Improving Experiences
Scale	Large	Smaller	One
Competition / Choice	None	Few	Many
Production Method	Mass Production	Batch Production (EOQ)	Mass Customization (1 to 1)
Marketing Method	Mass Marketing	Target Marketing	One to One Marketing
Selling Method	Transactional Selling	Consultative Selling	???? Selling

Advancements in transistor technology led to the development of the integrated circuit (1957). Tiny, silicon chips became home base for microscopic strips of metal working together to form the number-crunching logic centers of computers. The little chips worked faster than transistors, far faster than primitive vacuum tubes—and they kept getting faster and cheaper at a geometric rate. In the 1960's Intel founder Gordon Moore observed that every 18 months for the foreseeable future, the computing power of chips would double while cost stayed constant. As Moore's Law predicted, digital technology has continued to geometric decreases in size and increases in power.[2.4] Computers have changed from bulky, slow, and expensive machines that took up entire buildings to sleek, fast, and inexpensive devices that can be slipped in a shirt pocket.

This information crunching power and efficiency gave birth to the computer and software industries. The resulting tools and new methods enabled businesses to plan, work, learn, and communicate faster...and faster, until they took us over the *Just-In-Time Threshold*.

Just-in-Time technologies (tools and methods) began to create both the possibility and expectation of real-time development and delivery of personalized products and services.

Mass Customization

It is the age of Mass Customization—a paradox fewer than 20 years ago. Stan Davis first used the term 'mass customization' in his 1987 book <u>Future Perfect</u>. [2.5] Joseph Pine built on the thesis in his 1993 work, <u>Mass Customization</u>.[2.6] The goal of mass customization, according to Pine, is to develop, produce, market and deliver affordable goods with enough variety that nearly everyone finds exactly what he or she wants. Mass Customization means personalized products and mass produced efficiencies—made possible by digital technologies.

For the consumer, it means instead of choosing from identical mass-produced goods, or selecting from a smaller, specialized line, they now can design and order personalized products both on the Internet and in retail stores. Get measured for a custom fit pair of jeans at a GAP store in LA this morning. They're manufactured in Tennessee this afternoon. You receive them via FedEx by 10:30am tomorrow.

For companies, it means that speed, low cost, and personalization are no longer competitive advantages. They're requirements to stay in the game.

1:1 Marketing

Like production before it, as marketing entered the Digital Age, it completed the journey from targeting masses to niches to individuals.

<u>The One to One Future</u> by Don Peppers and Martha Rogers, Ph.D., formally introduced the concept of 1:1 marketing and a new vision statement for customer relationship management. "Relationships with individual customers, not target markets, will win the sales race today," Peppers and Rogers write. [2.7] 1:1 Marketing suggested a new paradigm that would not be possible without a platform for real-time interactive communication between companies and customers.

The development of digital technologies and the Internet made it both practical and possible. Marketers saw the opportunity to reach, learn about, and influence individual decision-makers and buying units—because individuals they were. Each person's preferences and purchases could be customized and compiled, tracked, and measured, in real time. Advertising messages could be personalized to create target markets of 1.

The growth of the information delivery industry has allowed consumers to shop and consume 24 hours a day, seven days a week. They could compare prices and performance ratings, as well as communicate with other consumers.

With information in abundance, low cost, high quality choices, and instant access were no longer competitive differences. They became new standards. As a result, corporations and salespeople watched their Information Age value propositions evaporate.

Selling in the Digital Age

As we have seen, Production (1980's) and Marketing (1990's) have crossed the digital divide and redefined how companies and customers do business in real time. But the current state-of-the-art for professional selling, consultative selling, is still stuck in the Information Age. Not for long.

As we enter the 21st century, our model suggests that now it's selling's turn to join the Digital Age!

	The Modern History of Selling		
	Machine Age	**Information Age**	**Digital Age**
Defining Technologies	Assembly Line	Transistor; Television	Integrated Circuit; Computers
Production Methods	Mass Production	Batch Production	Mass Customization
Marketing Methods	Mass Marketing	Target Marketing	One to One Marketing
Selling Methods	Transactional Selling	Consultative Selling	??? Selling

Why won't the current sales process paradigm, consultative selling, fit the bill? In the next chapter we'll take a look at what happens when you attempt to blend a traditional consultative 'high-touch' sales model with modern digital 'high-tech' tools.

CONSULTATIVE SELLING & TECHNOLOGY—A TALE OF WOE

Consultative selling is a method that came of age in the 1950's and '60's as an attempt to professionalize selling—and move it beyond its transactional 'sales pitch' image.

The Consultative Selling Process

Consultative selling is a five step process that includes: Building Rapport (Trust); Identifying Needs; Demonstrating Solutions; Managing Objections; and Closing the Sale. The innovation of consultative selling was the introduction of 'needs identification'—the orientation of the sales process around the client's goals and objectives.

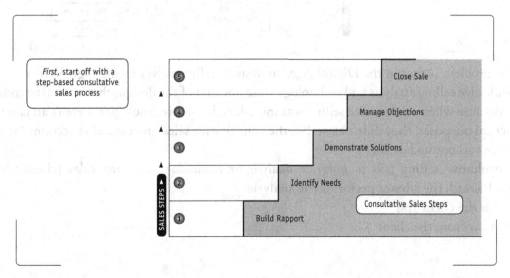

It redefined the salesperson as an expert *advisor* who was knowledgeable, objective and could be trusted. It shifted the role of salespeople from pitchmen to consultants who would identify clients' needs and guide them to a best-fit solution.

The Problem—A Hidden Sales Step

However, when used to sell complex products and services, such as financial planning, consultative selling suffers a fatal flaw because of a hidden step—*analysis*. Diagnosis, projections, and comparisons are just some of the examples of analysis that are integral to solving complex problems and selling complex products or services.

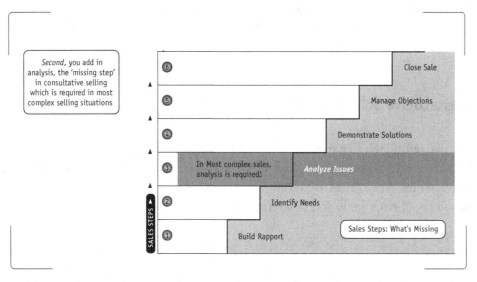

The problem is that in the Digital Age, analysis usually involves technology. When it comes to consultative selling analysis and technology were not part of the design, they're an afterthought. Why? Because when consultative selling was introduced, 'sales technologies' weren't an issue. For all practical purposes, they didn't exist. So, the consultative sales process didn't account for them and doesn't accommodate them.

Consultative selling *fails to integrate analysis* or technology into the sales (client-advisor) process. Instead, the advisor performs the analysis:

- for the client and
- away from the client

The standard practice is for salespeople to analyze issues in the privacy of their offices, out of client view, with the help of their computers and other resources, and return with a series of printouts or slideshows that are used as part of their sales presentation (for *demonstrating* solutions).

The Wizard of Oz Effect

We refer to the phenomenon that results as the Wizard of Oz Effect [3.1], or WOE, for short. After the client interview meeting, sales advisors disappear from client's view, like the Wizard of Oz behind the curtain, to consult their computers and prepare printouts and proposals, while their clients must go home, or back to their offices and wait.

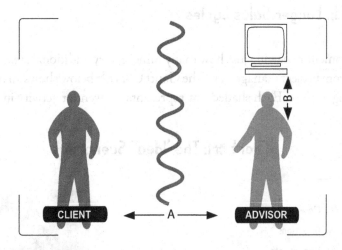

The picture above illustrates the two 'touches' involved that result in WOE: (A) the client interacts with the advisor, and (B) the advisor interacts with technology—away from the client.

And woe has greeted many sales advisors who came back to demonstrate their products and services with static graphics and spreadsheets only to discover they hadn't identified all of their clients' concerns, or anticipated their 'what if' questions. So, they go back to their computers and perform new analysis, while their client goes home, and waits—again...and again. In fact, almost any new information or changes send the Wizard back behind the curtain to perform additional analysis, delaying decisions, and sales—frustrating both clients and sales advisors.

WOE-ful Consequences

What are the results of WOE?

- Longer sales cycles
- Failure to recognize that clients do analysis too!
- Misunderstanding of customer 'objections'
- Decreased trust
- A poor customer experience

All of which reduce the likelihood of making a sale!!

WOE Results In Longer Sales Cycles

Let's spend a moment reviewing just how many unnecessary additional steps are caused by WOE. Taking a page from project management, the Gantt Chart [3.2] below shows all the Consultative Sales' steps from beginning to close. Each shaded box represents an event or activity in the sales process.

Chart #1: The 'Ideal' Scenario

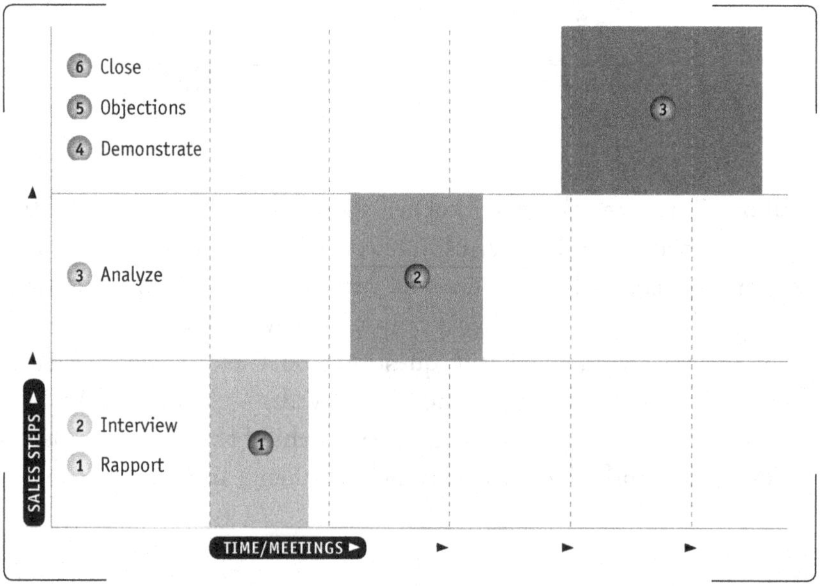

Chart #1 illustrates the 'Ideal' scenario. In their first meeting (Box 1), the client and salesperson meet to discuss the client's needs. The next planned meeting between them is the formal presentation (Box 3) that could also be the sales close. Between 1 & 3, there's our hidden step— when the salesperson must perform the analysis that becomes the basis of the demonstration.

This suggests a minimum 2-meeting, 3-step process.

Chart #2 represents the 'probable' or more likely case. If during the presentation, the client has questions that require new analysis ('What If?'), it's back to step 1 to get additional information and then the cycle starts all over. When we look at this chart, the implications are clear.

Chart #2: The More Likely Scenario

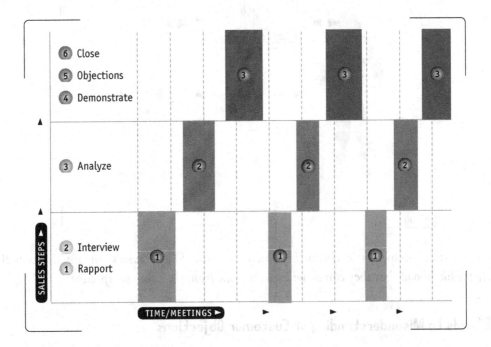

In sales situations involving complex products or services, where analysis is needed, consultative selling's process and traditional tools create gaps in time, decreasing the chance of completing a sale.

Each time new information or unanticipated questions are introduced, analysis is required. The sales process stops. The salesperson goes behind the curtain to create more printouts and, hopefully, picks up where they left off.

The more 'what ifs' raised …the more meetings…the longer the process…and the more likely the sale will derail entirely.

WOE Fails to Recognize That Clients Also Do Analysis

In the consultative model, analysis is the responsibility of the salesperson.

But do clients do analysis? Of course they do. With all the Digital Age resources at their disposal, it's likely that their tools are equal to the salesperson's. Delays give them opportunity and cause to do their own analysis.

Even worse, they are apt to relieve the tedium of waiting by consulting other sales advisors, and resolve the problem without you.

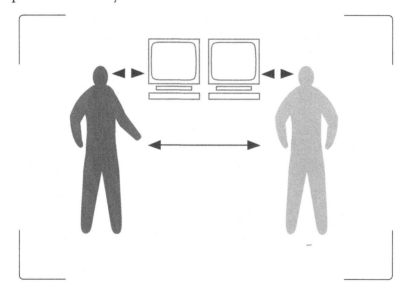

The client and salesperson each do their own analysis. The wizard's curtain works both ways, decreasing the likelihood that they can or will see the issue from the same perspective.

WOE Leads to Misunderstanding of Customer Objections

Salespeople are trained to manage or overcome 'objections'—client questions or changes that introduce delays in the sales process. This illustrates a fundamental misunderstanding of the real problem.

'What if' questions are a type of 'objection' that are a natural part of solving complex problems. In fact, as complexity goes up, so do customer 'what-ifs'. These questions demonstrate regression—a natural (and desirable) part of the learning cycle. [3.3] Complex problem resolution and decision-making can't occur without them. Trying to overcome, control, or manage these questions gets in the way of complex decision-making rather than speeding it up. That's why for some types of customer problems, the consultative sales process is very inefficient and therefore inappropriate.

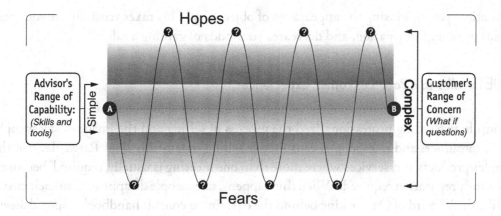

As complexity increases, so do 'what ifs'. The advisor's skills and tools play a vital role in helping people navigate these issues.

Why not embrace or even encourage objections instead? (Heresy!) There's a simple answer… salespeople have to 'overcome' objections when they don't have the capability (tools, skills, and methods) that allow them to explore and resolve them.

WOE Decreases Trust

Let's say you've met with your client, gathered information, and you take your leave to perform analysis and put together projections and presentations.

When you get back together, what's the first thing that happens? You and the client spend time reviewing and validating the inputs. You're describing what you did and why you did it. And they're looking for mistakes!

And unfortunately they're easy to find, because most software programs don't perfectly fit the data of your real-life case. When you're entering data, you must make assumptions, interpretations, and adjustments.

There is no such thing as perfect information! No matter how good of an interviewer you are, new information can (and inevitably will) appear that invalidates your current analysis and threatens the dreaded 'do-over.'

When working to build trust with a client, mistakes aren't the problem. Mistakes can demonstrate vulnerability which actually help build trust…as long as you recover from them quickly and effectively.

The real problem is that you have to send people away while you fix your 'mistakes'. You waste valuable time—both yours and the client's. If you try and explain away the issues to avoid this situation, you risk losing the appearance of objectivity. This taxes trust, limits your access to valuable customer information, and decreases your odds of gaining a sale.

WOE Results in a Poor Customer Experience

Consultative selling professionalized the process of selling and the image of salespeople. But for most consumers and salespeople, consultative selling is painfully *slow*. Particularly in the case of complex products and services where more than one meeting is usually 'required' because of the analysis and preparation required. When this happens, salespeople disappear from their customers' sight, like the Wizard of Oz working behind the curtain, to consult handbooks, spreadsheets, and other resources.

When they reappear, illustrations in hand, they hope they've hit their mark on the first try. However, if new information is presented or if the customer has questions for which the salesperson did not prepare, they must go back to the drawing board (computer), generate more illustrations, and setup yet another meeting. The more analysis required—the more meetings involved.

As authors Joseph Pine and James Gilmour pointed out in <u>The Experience Economy</u>[3.4] Digital Age competition is increasingly 'experience' and entertainment based. WOE leads to a frustrating string of meetings for both the customer and the salesperson. Given the many avenues that consumers face for their time and attention, sales advisors who are unable or unequipped to make the sales process a better experience for the customer will be replaced by those who can and do. There must be a better way.

The Great Consultative Cover-Up

And as you increase the time involved, and the amount of information you provide, you increase the risk involved in losing a now informed prospect to your competition.

There are a lot of good salespeople who avoid using technology or implementing a true consultative planning approach as a result. Instead, they come in with a couple of suggestions they understand, can support, and can close. What you end up with is a consultative selling 'veneer', on a product/service selling core—consultative in image but not in fact.

Companies struggle to reconcile the importance of a consultative sales approach, while realizing and hiding the fact that most of their best salespeople don't really do it. In turn, this makes it harder to get other people to do it and build a true consultative selling approach into the culture.

According to noted sales-author and researcher George Dudley:

"When examined closely, much of the consultative sales training today is actually a cover, not a cure, for the underlying ambivalence, conflictedness, and sometimes unbridled contempt, many salespeople and their organizations actually hold for the sales profession itself (Chonko, Tanner & Dudley, 2003). In other words, it's *meta-selling*: a set of convoluted attempts and diversionary tactics to elevate selling by disguising or minimizing the role of the sales effort. So far, research has not been kind to subtext underlying many diversionary selling programs. Something else may be needed." [3.5]

This is why we suggest that consultative selling is just a kinder, gentler version of transactional selling, and merely a transitional step in the evolution of professional selling. It's a step in the right direction, but it's incomplete.

But advances in sales technology and processes are taking place that will help salespeople take the next step in the evolution of selling and establish it as the new paradigm for selling in the Digital Age.

SELLING—THE NEXT GENERATION

What's the Next Step?

What will the new selling method look like? Our shared history model provides a clue.

The Modern History of Selling		
	Machine Age	**Information Age**	**Digital Age**
Defining Technologies	Assembly Line	Transistor; Television	Integrated Circuit; Computers
Production Method	Mass Production	Batch Production	Mass Customization
Marketing Method	Mass Marketing	Target Marketing	One to One Marketing
Selling Method	Transactional Selling	Consultative Selling	??? Selling
Approach	Impersonal	↔	Personal
Speed	Slower	↔	Faster

The final step in the evolution of selling requires an approach that is faster and provides a better customer experience without sacrificing personal touch or professionalism!

Companies spend billions of dollars annually to help them improve market share (selling to more people) and wallet share (selling more to each person). But when everyone is gunning for the same customers both have natural limits. The new competitive landscape that will redefine profitable competition will be *time-share*: reducing sales-cycle time (i.e., result in selling *faster*). Companies and salespeople that can't sell both fast and professionally will be at a significant competitive disadvantage to those that can. [4.1]

The challenge of selling in the Digital Age will be to learn and adapt to the requirements of *fast-professional* selling. Those who take up the challenge and gain new skills will be greatly rewarded, both financially and with their customers' respect. Those who can't adapt will suffer the same fate as Willy Loman, bypassed by a world that has evolved beyond their outdated skills and sales techniques.

The Fast-Professional Paradox

But…how can *salespeople* sell both fast *and* professionally?

It's easy to imagine selling faster using Kiosks or Internet e-commerce—transactional technologies that usually take the sales/service person out of the process. E-commerce and other technology automated systems are very fast, but not very personal. How do you sell faster with people in the process?

When it comes to professional selling, a transactional approach is *fast*. A 30-second demonstration in a supermarket aisle, or a three-minute telemarketer's pitch will get the job done for some types of products and services. But it is not suited for *professional* selling.

Consultative selling is *professional and personal*, but not very fast. In fact, in the majority of cases it is *painfully* slow. Particularly in the case of complex products and services where multiple meetings are needed of the analysis and preparation required.

For years, companies and salespeople have been trying to find a bridge between these two worlds (speed and professionalism) with limited success. What's made this particularly frustrating for companies is the challenge of balancing their simultaneous desires for faster sales and elevating the image of salespeople from pitchman to trusted sales advisors.

Like trying to fix a leaky roof in the middle of a rainstorm, it has resulted in an almost endless list of quick fixes (and rationalizations for why they haven't worked). Fast-professional selling…is it even possible? As we enter the 21st century, the answer has arrived—*just in time*. [4.2]

Just-in-Time Or...In Due Time?

In the Digital Age, old paradoxes have become the new paradigms. The adoption of Digital Age tools and methods brought JIT to manufacturing in the 1980s, to marketing in the 1990s, and now it's selling's turn. If Mass-Customization is JIT production and 1:1 Marketing is JIT marketing...then the new model for selling in the Digital Age should be a *JIT Selling approach.* Simple enough! But what is JIT selling?

Let's take another look at our consultative sales Gantt Chart to see how this might work. As the chart illustrates, a professional consultative sales approach that involves analysis requires three separate events and provides a best-case scenario of two meetings to reach a possible conclusion or sale. (Chart A).

Chart A

Events/Meetings Involved

Events	Activities
1	*Meeting #1.* Prospects and salespeople meet so the salesperson can *develop rapport and gather information.*
2	*Planning.* Then prospect leaves and is made to 'wait' while the salesperson *does analysis and prepares something to present.*
3	*Meeting #2.* When they meet again, the salesperson *demonstrates the proposed solutions* they created while away from the prospect—hoping that the initial interview and analysis were thorough enough to address all of the prospect's concerns.

If everything goes according to plan, business is transacted. As we saw in the last chapter, any questions or changes that require new analysis send us back to the drawing board and the cycle starts over—introducing delays in the form of additional meetings and plans as illustrated in Chart B.

Chart B

So what should salespeople do in sales situations where analysis is required? Accept the inevitable delays, lost sales, and lousy customer experience that result...or find a better way?

⭐ Integrating the Sales Steps

Why do these need to be separate events? What if...we could bring all three steps together, including analysis? Just for a moment, I want you to suspend any disbelief you might have over whether it's possible or practical. (We'll demonstrate the *'why'* in Part III of this book and the *'how'* in Part IV.)

If we could accomplish this, we would theoretically collapse the time required for professional selling to a single meeting resulting in a sales picture that looks like Chart C below.

Chart C

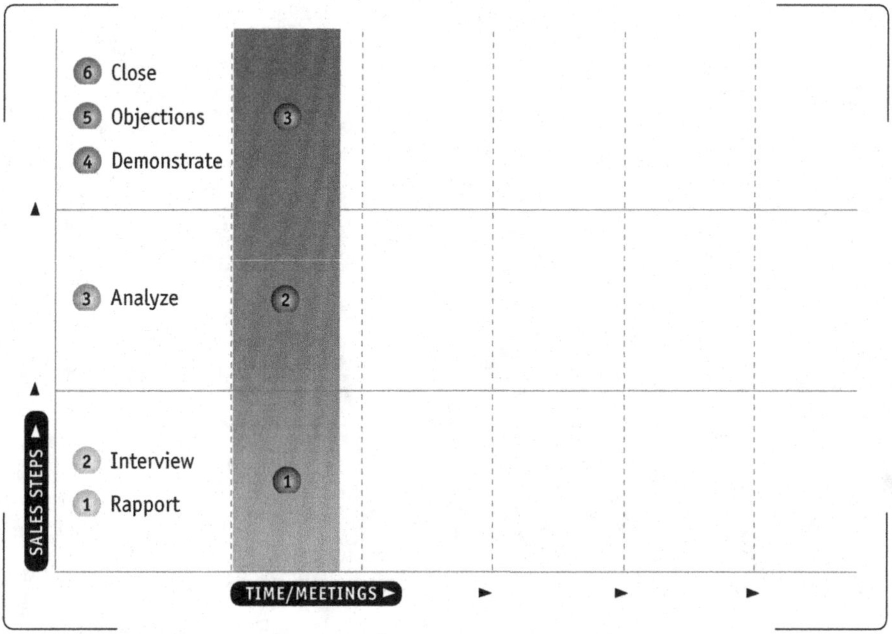

By eliminating unnecessary delays, salespeople and customers could move seamlessly between the sales steps to identify problems, present solutions, make decisions, and take action *in real time.* [4.3] While this sounds great in theory, how do you do it in the real world?

How Do We Do It?

If we can apply JIT to production and marketing, why can't we apply it to selling?

We can, but instead of patching the leaky consultative selling roof, we need to rebuild it. By **reengineering** the consultative sales process (thoughtfully breaking and rebuilding it around Digital Age technologies), just-in-time professional selling can be achieved. And the results, like production and marketing before it, will include increased efficiency, productivity, *and quality* that create greater value for customers, companies, and salespeople.

In Part 3 of the book, *Reengineering the Sales Process,* we'll take on this effort.

REENGINEERING THE SALES PROCESS

Part III
Part III
Part III
Part III

INTRODUCTION

"If there is a way to do it better... find it."
—Thomas Edison

Part II of this book was about selling's past and present. We talked about how technological advances are removing salespeople from the selling process. In particular, we talked about WOE (the Wizard of Oz Effect): how and why technology 'interferes' with the traditional consultative selling process. We finished by considering how to eliminate the WOE that results when planning tools and analysis are needed in a professional sales process. Our history of selling model provided the clue—Just-In-Time. Now an old paradox is about to become a new paradigm—fast-professional selling.

What's required for fast-professional selling? The tools that are the current industry standards aren't designed for it and won't facilitate it. The current sales paradigm of consultative selling won't accommodate it.

The way most people sell with technology today is 'broken' and unless we 'fix' it, advances in selling technologies will simply continue to take people out of the process. Selling fast and professionally requires a fundamental redesign of sales tools and processes.

In Part III—Reengineering the Sales Process—we take on the task of fixing it. In the process, not only will we describe why the development of a new sales method is inevitable, we'll demonstrate why it's imperative.

BUILDING A NEW FOUNDATION

Reengineering Described

What's involved in our rebuilding process? Let's take a look at the definition of Reengineering[5.1] for clues.

> *"Reengineering is the fundamental rethinking and radical redesign of business processes to achieve dramatic improvements in critical, contemporary measures of performance, such as cost, quality, service, and speed."* From <u>Reengineering the Corporation</u> by Dr. Michael Hammer

This definition has five key concepts in it:

- *Fundamental*—Reengineering takes nothing for granted. It ignores what is and concentrates on what should be. It starts with the most basic questions. Why do we do what we do? And why do we do it that way?
- *Radical*—Reengineering is about reinvention—not merely improvement, enhancement, or modification of what already exists. Reengineering means tossing aside old systems and starting over. It involves going back to the beginning and inventing a better way of doing work.
- *Dramatic*—Reengineering isn't about making marginal or incremental improvements, but about achieving quantum leaps in performance. Marginal improvement requires fine-tuning; dramatic improvement demands blowing up the old and replacing it with something new.
- *Processes*—Reengineering involves changing processes (wholes) not simply tasks and activities (parts).
- *Critical Contemporary Measures*—Individual tasks and activities are important, but none of them matters if the overall process doesn't deliver the desired results such as speed, quality, productivity, and service.

SELL (from Old English, sellen, to give, to deliver; to hand over): To exchange or deliver for money or its equivalent; to offer for sale, as for one's business or livelihood

BUY (from Old English, buggen, to acquire): To acquire in exchange for money or its equivalent; purchase; to acquire by the payment of a price or value; -- opposed to sell.

So where do we begin? We need to go back to the fundamentals. So let's start by reconsidering the purpose of selling and salespeople.

What Is Selling Anyway?

Let's step back and take a look and see what we mean by selling.

Selling as a Set of Activities and Tasks

When most people think of selling, they think of the activities involved. As you can see from the dictionary definitions on the left, there's very little difference between the *terms* selling and buying.

You could say that selling and buying are the same thing—only that they are seen from different perspectives. It depends on whose shoes we're standing in when a transaction takes place—the buyers or the sellers?

To get a better understanding of how selling takes place, let's look at a process definition.

Selling as a Scientific Process

"The important thing in science is not so much to obtain new facts as to discover new ways of thinking about them."—Sir William Bragg

Selling is a process that involves:
1. Identifying issues that require attention;
2. Clarifying the current circumstances in which the problem exists (the current scenario);
3. Considering possible alternative situations/scenarios that may be preferred;
4. Choosing among the alternatives;
5. Setting goals; and
6. Designing suitable courses of action.

In Decision Science[5.2], the first three of these activities are usually called *problem-solving*; the last three are called *decision-making*.

Professional Selling Involves	
PROBLEM SOLVING	**DECISION-MAKING**
Choosing issues that require attention	Choosing among the alternatives
Clarifying the current circumstances (scenario) in which the problem exists	Setting goals
Considering possible alternative situations that may be preferred	Designing suitable courses of action

The value of defining selling this way, as a problem-solving and decision-making process, is that we can utilize over a half century of research in psychology, economics, and management science to help make selling more scientific.

What does this give us? Consider what being scientific suggests. Scientific explanations must meet certain criteria:

- Observable
- Measurable
- Repeatable
- Transferable

Making selling more scientific paves the way for improving both the experience and the outcome for customers and salespeople. It also helps us move away from the image of selling as a black art, and towards an understanding of the skills, knowledge, and development process anyone can acquire—not just 'born salespeople.'

Selling as a Social Science

What *type* of science is selling?

Selling is a *social science* that describes the interactions between people as buying and selling takes place.

What do we mean by a social science? As the definitions to the left illustrate, social sciences deal with relationships between people and attempt to describe how individuals interact with each other and society.

Why is it important to make this distinction? Because the methods and tools of the social sciences are different from those of the physical sciences. They are qualitative as well as quantitative. Does this mean they are less 'scientific'?

The very nature of social science is changing as the understanding of human behavior becomes more firmly grounded in science. This can be seen in advances in neurology, studies of the brain, etc., that are bridging the gap between 'exact' sciences and social science.

We suggest that looking at *psychology, economics*, and *management science* can help provide a clearer picture of the 'science of selling'. [5.3]

How is selling like psychology?

Psychology is defined as the scientific study of behavior and underlying mental processes. Psychologists study the "ABC's" of a person (a=affects or emotions, b=behaviors, c=cognition or thoughts). They seek to understand why we think, act, and feel as we do. Psychologists conduct both basic research (research done to enhance knowledge and scientific understanding) and applied research (research done to solve a practical problem) in their efforts to understand behavior and mental processes.

Like psychology:

- Selling is a study of human motives and behaviors
- Selling is a helping profession

How is selling like economics?

Economics is a social science that studies how societies distribute goods, services and resources. Microeconomics is a branch of economics that studies the behavior of small economic units, such as that of individual consumers or households. Microeconomics is also referred to as price theory because it studies supply and demand and the decision tradeoffs that result in price.

Selling is like economics because it:

- Describes the tradeoffs that occur that lead to buying and selling decisions
- Studies the relationship between price and perceived customer value

How is selling like management science?

Management science (also referred to as operations research, quantitative methods, quantitative analysis, and decision sciences) is the application of a scientific approach to solving management problems in order to help managers make better decisions. It encompasses a number of mathematically oriented techniques that have either been developed within the field of management science or been adapted from other disciplines, such as the natural sciences, mathematics, statistics, and engineering.

Management science is a recognized and established discipline in the field of business administration. The applications of management science are widespread, and they have been frequently credited with increasing the efficiency and productivity of business firms.

Like management science:

- Selling is a decision science
- A scientific evaluation of selling helps explain how we can make the process more efficient and effective. It helps provide a framework for understanding how to improve the selling process.

If we're trying to improve efficiency, why not just take salespeople out of the process completely? Couldn't all the steps be completed by the consumer alone without an extra person in the process?

While it may seem intuitively obvious that salespeople must provide value if they're going to be included in the process...how exactly do you *create* value?

In the next section, we'll see how salespeople create value as we develop 'first principles' for the science of selling.

Establishing Scientific First Principles

Value is a fairly subjective and ethereal concept. To provide a working definition and some basic rules for creating value, we paraphrased a section from Michael Hammer's book, <u>Beyond Reengineering</u>. [5.4] In a chapter titled *Why a Business?*, Dr. Hammer, a PhD physicist and leading management consultant, suggests three scientific 'first principles' as a guide for understanding how a business and its people create value.

According to Hammer, the three 'first principles' of business are:

1. *The mission of a business is to create value for a customer.* Value is not synonymous with a product or service, although it often involves one or both. Rather, value in a business context means a solution to a customer's problem. It is whatever it takes to answer a customer's need, to scratch a customer's itch.

2. *It is a company's processes that create value for its customers.* We define a process as a complete end-to-end set of activities or tasks that together create value for a customer. The tasks are the bits of work that people actually perform, but the tasks themselves do not create value nor do the individuals performing them. It is only whole processes, all the tasks put together, that create value.

3. *Business success comes from superior process performance.* This principle follows from the first two. If our purpose is to create value and our processes create that value, then better processes will do it better.

Simply stated, the first three principles suggest that:

- Companies provide value by solving customer problems.
- It's their processes that provide this resolution and create customer value.
- Business success and greater value are the result of effective process performance.

The language and logic illustrate the link between Problems, Processes, and Performance. How do you get superior performance? Performance requires more than just execution...it requires proper alignment. There must be an appropriate match between problem and process.

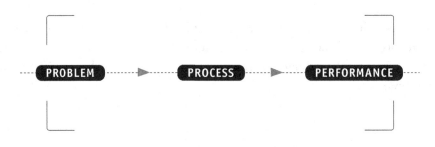

When problems and processes are properly aligned and executed, you get greater value and performance. When there's a mismatch between problems and the processes used to solve them, ineffective performance and reduced value are the results.

While this problem→process→performance model was designed for management, it translates easily into sales principles that provide a framework for understanding the purpose of selling and the roles that salespeople play in the process.

How Do Salespeople Create Value?

To see how this applies to selling, let's re-frame these management principles as sales principles:

- Salespeople create value by helping customers solve problems.
- Salespeople create value for companies and customers through their processes.
- Sales success is the result of superior sales process performance.

This helps us explain why the value that salespeople create, and their reason for being, isn't simply based on the type of products they sell...or the type of people they sell to. It's also based on the *type of problem* the client is faced with.

We believe this gets to the root cause of the greatest challenge facing salespeople and the selling profession in the 21st century. Technological advances have provided customers many new ways to solve problems. For many of the problems customers face, salespeople aren't a necessary part of the process. Can salespeople be replaced? The answer is yes—for some, but not all *types of problems*.

To get a clearer picture of this, let's look at what we mean by different types of problems.

WHAT'S YOUR PROBLEM?

"There are no more promising or important targets for basic scientific research than understanding how human minds, with and without the help of computers, solve problems and make decisions effectively, and improving our problem-solving and decision-making capabilities."
—Herbert Simon, Nobel Prize Winner

What kinds of problems do people face and how are they different?

Understanding the definitions and the differences between the different problem types is important because as we'll see...

* Different types of problems suggest different methods and tools to solve them.
* Match them appropriately and greater value is created.
* When they are mismatched, value is decreased.

The analysis provided in this chapter will help illustrate what types of problems people need help with and, as a result, where salespeople create the greatest value.

The model that follows provides a useful framework for this discussion.

The TOP (Type of Problem) Model

There are many ways to describe problems. We chose the following three measures (or dimensions) that are commonly used in psychology and management science to help classify problems as different types:

1. Information vs. Experience
2. Certainty vs. Risk
3. Linear vs. Non-linear

First, we'll describe each of these dimensions and then we'll give the four TOP [6.1] problem types that they suggest names and descriptions.

Dimension #1: Information vs. Experience

All problems require varying degrees of information and experience to be applied to them in order to resolve them.

Problem Types Classified by Information and Experience

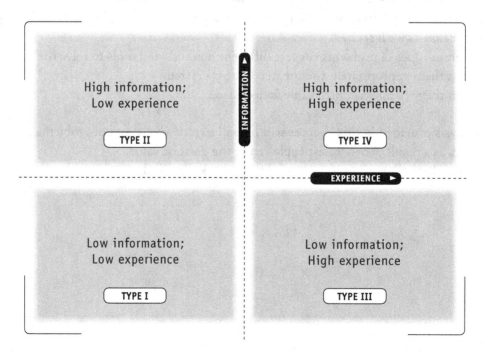

The picture suggests four basic problem types that result from combining different levels of information and experience:

- Type I: Low information, Low experience
- Type II: High information, Low experience
- Type III: Low information, High experience
- Type IV: High information, High experience

Dimension #2: Certainty vs. Risk

In the fields of Computer and Decision Sciences, decisions are typically classified as being one of three types: [6.2]

- Decisions Under Certainty
- Decisions At Risk
- Decisions Under Uncertainty

What's the difference? Let's suppose we have a choice between two actions. We're in the realm of:

- *Certainty* if each action has a set of known outcomes.
- *Risk* if either action has a set of possible outcomes each with a known probability.
- *Uncertainty* if either action has unknowable outcomes or probabilities.

We use these definitions to create our second problem type dimension: ***Certainty vs. Risk.***

In our use: *Uncertainty* provides us with a spectrum from Low (known probabilities) to High Uncertainty (unknown probabilities). *Risk* means the number of possible outcomes with High Risk suggesting more possible outcomes and Low Risk suggesting fewer.

Problem Types Classified by Certainty and Risk

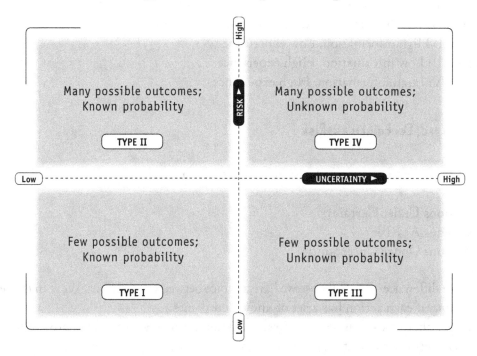

The chart then provides us with two different ways to evaluate the likelihood or predictability of events.

Dimension #3: Linear vs. Non-linear

Our third category for classifying problems is **Linearity**. What do we mean by linearity? *Something is linear if it changes in a regular way or direction (i.e., a story's linear development from beginning to end).*

Linearity provides us a graphic way to illustrate the different problem types. What does linearity look like? Consider the definition of a **Linear Equation**: *An equation with solutions that lie on a straight line when they are placed on a graph.* The graphics in the next table help explain how linearity applies to each of the problem types.

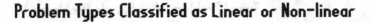

Problem Types Classified as Linear or Non-linear

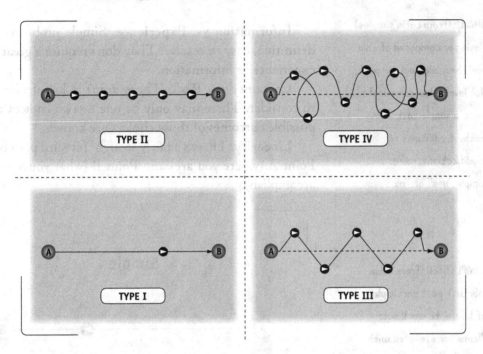

What do the pictures suggest? The dots or small arrows that you see in each picture suggest points of consideration: things that must be evaluated or considered in the problem/decision process. The more dots—the more things to consider.

The shape or path of the line in each picture suggests the relative orderliness of the solution process. So, problem types I & II, as we've defined them, are more appropriately solved by logical linear-thinking approaches than problem types III & IV.

Now, with our three dimensions in place, (1. *Information vs. Experience*; 2. *Certainty vs. Risk*; and 3. *Linear vs. Nonlinear*), let's give the problem types they suggest proper names and descriptions.

Problem Type Descriptions

The following definitions provide a quick overview of problem types. The table at the end of the section compares them. (We'll cover types III & IV in more detail in upcoming chapters on understanding and managing complexity.)

Type I Problems Are Simple Problems [6.3]

Information vs. Experience. Simple problems are, by definition, easy to resolve. They don't require a great deal of experience or information.

Certainty vs. Risk. There aren't a lot of alternatives to consider. There may only be one or two choices and the possible outcomes of those choices are known.

Linearity. There's a fairly straight forward path between Point A (where you are) and Point B (what you're trying to accomplish).

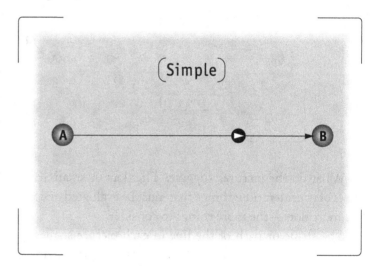

Useful Metaphor: A no-brainer.

Sales Implications. People typically don't need other people to help them solve simple problems. Then, what types of problems do people typically seek help for? Difficult ones obviously!

The next three definitions (problem types II, III, & IV) will describe types of problems that people typically consider more *difficult*: problems that they either won't or can't resolve on their own.

"Make everything as simple as possible, but not simpler."
—Albert Einstein

Type II Problems Are Complicated Problems [64]

Information vs. Experience.

Complicated, as we define it, is synonymous with *elaborate* or detailed.

Solving complicated problems typically requires book smarts: greater information or education than required by simple problems.

Linearity. As the picture below illustrates, getting from Point A to Point B requires more information (dots—things to know or consider).

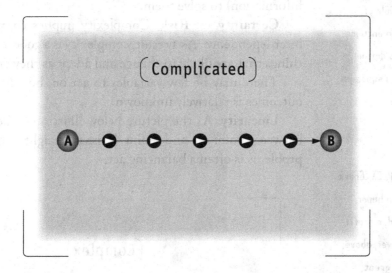

Certainty vs. Risk. Complicated problems have either known or knowable probabilities to their outcomes.

Useful Metaphor. Rocket science. There is much to know, but it can be learned through observation and study.

Sales Implications. Tech-savvy consumers, who can gain access to specialized information with just a click or two on the Internet, are quickly making professionals who make a living off providing information obsolete.

For example, in the 'old' days, pre-Internet, a patent attorney might have been needed to answer a question about a patent application or to find out the availability or status of a trademark. Today, a person can get answers to many of these questions directly from the U.S. Patent Office's Web site (www.uspto. gov)—another example of information expertise and billable hours give way to the Internet's speed and convenience.

COMPLEX (from the Latin "complexus"): the word complex means to embrace or "being composed of a multitude of objects"; past participle of complect, to entwine. We chose to define complex as a synonym of intricate.

HYPER-COMPLEX (Greek huper): from huper, over, beyond; a prefix signifying over, above; abnormally great, excessive)

Type III Problems Are Complex Problems [6.4]

The dictionary definitions of complicated and complex are similar. Both describe problems that are difficult to analyze…for different reasons.

The differences may appear subtle but they are substantial.

Information vs. Experience. Complex problems require street smarts rather than book smarts (experience rather than information) to solve them.

Certainty vs. Risk. Complexity implies connectedness and interdependence. As a result, complexity is a good word to describe things that are likely to change and adapt as they are acted on.

There may be few variables to act on, but the probability of outcomes is relatively unknown.

Linearity. As the picture below illustrates, the solution path between Point A and Point B isn't straight. Solving complex problems is often a balancing act.

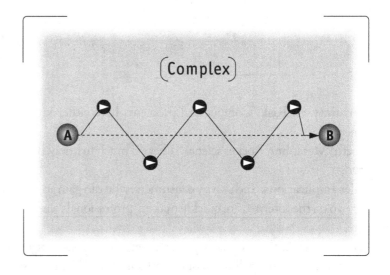

Life is becoming more complex.

Useful Metaphor. A balancing act. For example, you can't learn to ride a bicycle by reading about it. You must experience the feeling of being on the bicycle, and learn to continue rolling forward while not falling sideways.

Sales Implications. In complex sales situations, decisions are based more on experience than on logic. For example, it's easier to sell a sports car by taking someone for a test drive than it is by citing statistics.

Type IV Problems Are Hyper-Complex Problems[6.5]

Information vs. Experience. Hyper-complex problems represent a special class of highly complex problems that are difficult to solve without a high degree of information *and* experience. They require both book smarts and street smarts. One or the other alone won't suffice.

Take heart surgery, for example. Would you rather have a surgeon who graduated from a top school (education) or someone who had performed hundreds of successful surgeries (experience)? Most would want a surgeon with both.

Certainty vs. Risk. There are a greater number of possible outcomes, with the probability of the outcomes unknowable.

Linearity. As the graph below illustrates, the solution path isn't straight and where you're located may not be intuitively obvious.

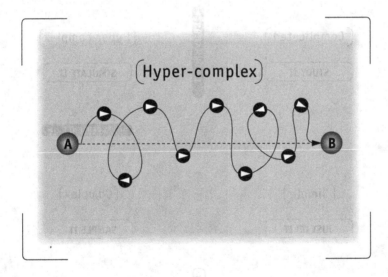

Useful Metaphor. Flying an airplane. There's a reason why there is both classroom and flight time required to become a professional pilot. One or the other is not enough. For example, when flying an airplane, a pilot's senses tell him the plane is flying straight when it is actually pulling to the right. Technologies that provide objective feedback are critical. Professional pilots must have an instrument rating that demonstrates their expertise in understanding the feedback technology gives them. Intuition alone is not enough. You have to learn to trust your instruments and understand how to interpret them.

Implication. When you're dealing with hyper-complex problems, you need feedback systems that will help overcome the natural failures of human intuition involved.

How Do You Handle The Different Problem Types?

What are appropriate ways to handle each of these different types of problems?

While there may be many different ways, the table below offers broad common-sense suggestions. These examples are not intended to be precise scientific descriptions. Instead they are relatively accurate observations that are useful for our discussion because they help illustrate key differences between the left side of the table (types I & II) and the right side of the table (types III & IV).

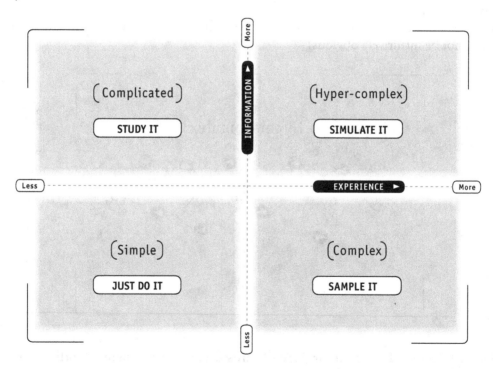

Type I: Simple Problems. What's the suggested resolution? When you're dealing with a simple problem, don't study it, sample it, or simulate it. Just do it.

Type II: Complicated Problems. What about complicated problems? Study them. Research them. Get out the manual. Either become an expert resource or go find one to help you.

Type III: Complex Problems. When dealing with complexity, information is less valuable and experience has greater value. So how do you solve complex problems? Sample. Experiment. Learn from your own experience or find someone who has 'been there and done that.'

There are many types of problems that can be resolved through actions, research, and experimentation. But for some types of problems, it's simply not prudent to act without planning; it's not possible to solve them through study; and it's not practical to learn from experience. That provides a good description of hyper-complex problems.

Type IV: Hyper-complex Problems. When dealing with hyper-complexity, resolving problems typically results from vicarious experiences: learning from other people's experiences or finding some way to play out possible alternatives without actually going through them.

Problem Types Compared

The following table provides a quick summary of the four problem types.

Why is it so important to illustrate and explain these differences?

Because there is a fundamental shift taking place that is increasing the number of *Complex* and *Hyper-Complex* problems people face... *life is becoming more complex!*

Life in the 21st century involves more choices for consumers; more competition for companies; and changes that occur faster and more unpredictably due to advances in technology.

Problem Types				
DESCRIPTION	SIMPLE	COMPLICATED	COMPLEX	HYPER-COMPLEX
Required Experience	Low	Low	High	High
Required Information	Low	High	Low	High
Required Skills	Logic	Education	Experience	Education + Experience
Number of Variables	Few	Many	Few	Many
Solutions Process	Linear	Linear	Non-Linear	Non-Linear
Solutions Process (Graphic)	(Simple)	(Complicated)	(Complex)	(Hyper-complex)
Problem Resolution	Just Do It	Study It	Sample It	Simulate It

In this chapter, we provided a basic overview of the problem types and appropriate methods for resolving them. In the next two chapters, we'll go into greater detail on appropriate ways to help people understand and manage complex and hyper-complex problems.

117

UNDERSTANDING COMPLEXITY

"Many of the difficult problems we face are caused by the difference between the way that nature works and how people think."
—Gregory Bateson

In the chapter on Types of Problems we gave a 'quick' description of complexity. In this chapter, we're going to go deeper to clarify why it's so important.

Why Is Complexity Important?

Increasing Complexity. As we suggested at the end of the last chapter, instability driven by increasing change, competition, and choice is the inevitable reality for business in the 21st century. As a result, the world and the problems facing most people are becoming increasingly complex.

Providing Real Value. Simply stated—most clients don't need salespeople to help them with simple problems! Many of the 'hard' problems that drive prospects and clients to work with an advisor are *complex*.

Are You Helping or Hurting? When you're trying to help a client deal with complex problems and decisions, you can do more harm than good unless you understand and can manage the underlying issues involved. Understanding complexity and knowing how to manage it are key skills for problem solving and selling in the 21st century.

Why Is It So Hard?

It's Not Simple Stupid

Most people struggle with understanding the behavior of complex-systems issues.

People usually try simplifying them to understand, explain, and then solve them…often with unexpected and undesirable results.

This points to a failure of logic and traditional 'strategic' approaches in dealing with complex problems.

To properly understand the behavior of complex systems, we need to take a closer look.

Complexity Defined

There's another definition of complexity that provides a powerful insight into how to understand and manage it.

Complexity describes systems behavior. [7.1]

What do we mean by systems? A system is a group of interacting, interrelated, or interdependent elements forming a complex whole.

Where do we find them? Systems are everywhere. Examples of systems include: economic systems; political systems; social systems; work groups; teams; families; and relationships.

What is systems behavior? Groups of people provide a good example. It's obvious that groups of people work differently together than they do separately. Why? Because when they work together what each person does separately affects how every other person in the group acts.

How do we see systems behavior in problems and decisions? To get a better understanding of how this applies to problems and decisions, let's look at the characteristics of complex systems.

Characteristics of Complex Systems

Interdependent issues; multiple parties or variables involved; issues that adapt and change over time; delays between cause and effect; a combination of emotional and logical issues going on…This is the nature of complex problems. [7.2]

The Learning Challenge

One of the defining factors of complex problems is separation between cause and effect. Cause and effect relationships in complex problems are often not clear. The more complex a problem is, the more difficult it is to picture how changing any one of its variables might alter the outcome. When cause and effect are separated in time or clarity, it's harder for people to learn from experience.

"When cause and effect are separated by time, people are notoriously poor learners."—Peter Senge

Traditional Approaches Don't Work

Dealing with complex problems is often difficult and frustrating. The results of applying conventional solutions are often poor enough to create discouragement from continuing or even trying.

Counter-Intuitive

As a result, our intuition about the outcomes of complex problems is often flawed. Although intuition can help us speculate on what might happen, using intuition alone to solve complex problems can lead to disaster.

Counter-Analytical

The analytical process that works for solving complicated problems often backfires when trying to solve complex problems due to unintended consequences.

Complicated problems can be dissected by studying them. Complex problems are difficult to break into parts. As a result, they are difficult to solve using logic alone.

Resolving complex problems often requires people to deal with difficult tradeoffs. Complex issues are not easily translated into static models, like reports and ledgers because they aren't easily broken into parts without losing a sense of the whole.

Counter to the Way Most People Are Trained

The academic, professional, and cultural training we've received for most of our lives has not equipped us to handle complex problems. In fact, it often works against our ability to solve them.

Complex problems require us to think differently. Understanding and managing complexity requires the ability to look at the big picture: to consider problems holistically and to consider the impact of decisions today on future events.

Future Focus

When people make decisions about the future, they often use the past as a guide.

Important questions about the future are usually too complex or imprecise for the conventional languages of business and science. Since complexity and uncertainty have emerged as driving forces in the way the world works, the belief in quantifiable truth and reliable prediction, the foundations of strategic planning, has begun to give way.

Strategic planning is a structured method that uses the past to help predict the future. Perhaps that approach worked well when the scope of decisions was relatively small and events were relatively predictable. But in a world of increasing complexity and uncertainty, a new approach is required.

 **Complexity and Decision-Making**

Typical Responses

When people are faced with complex problems, common responses are to:
- Add more information
- Attempt to simplify by breaking it down (taking away information)
- Freeze and do nothing

- Experiment to see what will happen
- Put a band-aid on it
- Jump in or out—at the wrong time
- Try anything and declare the first thing that worked the solution

As a result, complex problems often result in people responding in inappropriate simple ways and getting unexpected and undesirable results.

Atypical Results

Adding more information doesn't clear up a complex problem...and it can easily lead to analysis paralysis. More analysis doesn't help, because you can't *think* your way through complex problems, you have to *learn* your way through them.

Taking away information and oversimplifying the problem doesn't solve it either. *KISS:* The 'Keep It Simple Stupid' philosophy originates from a fundamental misunderstanding of the nature of complex problems. When you're trying to solve complex problems, you have to start by looking at the big picture, not by adding up the small pieces. When you're dealing with complexity, KISS provides short-term solutions that only mask the underlying problem.

Other typical responses also yield atypical results. What are some other common sense examples? Phrases like 'cutting off your nose to spite your face', 'penny wise and pound foolish', and 'fixes that backfire' illustrate an understanding of simple actions and unintended consequences.

Navigating Through Complexity

The decision-making process for hyper-complex problems can be compared to the course of a plane on autopilot. Autopilot works to correct the plane as it moves away from its flight path, which is plotted as a straight line. The plane is never flying in a perfectly straight line. The flight path looks more like a series of curves intersecting with a line. The average of these course deviations and corrections brings the plane to its destination. The flight of the plane on autopilot can be seen as the successful result of intentional trial and error.

This is similar to the process people go through as they make complex decisions. (Refer to the 'Navigating Complexity' graphic on the following page.) On their decision flight path, people move back and forth between hopes and fears. Hope inspires experimentation and progression. Fear inhibits action and promotes regression (taking a step back). But like a plane flying on autopilot, the learning process suggests that a person will go off course both ways as they move towards their desired destination.

Navigating Complexity: Hopes and Fears

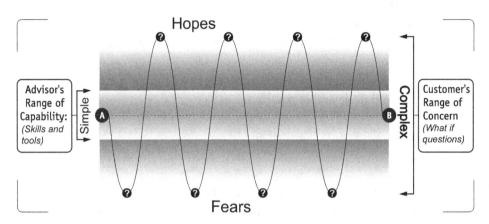

How do people generally view the decision process? In the rear view mirror. By results, not process. In hindsight, the decision may look simple or linear—but how they actually got there was not.

Complexity and Selling

Complexity and the Traditional Sales Process

Traditional sales tools and methods are inappropriate for complex problem solving and decision-making because…

Words Aren't Effective. When you're trying to explain these issues to customers, it's easy for them to get lost in the maze of information and for messages to get lost in translation. When communicating complex problems and issues to clients…*written words and verbal explanations generally aren't effective.* What alternatives are there? Instead of telling them the answer—try showing them.

Pictures Aren't Enough. They say 'a picture is worth a thousand words.' That's because pictures are better tools for communicating complex information than words. Ears work at the speed of sound and eyes work at the speed of light. Of all the senses, the visual pathway has the greatest bandwidth to and influence over the brain. Visual is like a T-1 line…direct and fast. It makes sense that if we could *show* someone the answers to complex problems, it would probably be a faster and more effective way than trying to tell them the answers.

But pictures including graphs, charts, and printouts are static. Your clients' understanding of the issues is not. As you provide more information, their understanding expands. Once clients begin to understand the issues, what-if questions and new information usually result requiring *changes* in your pictures. You end up going back and doing it over...and over. That's why *pictures aren't enough.*

Conventional Sales Tools Get in the Way. Most sales tools are designed for creating static presentations (either slideshows or printouts) that are not easily changed. They are not designed for the iteration required by addressing client follow-up questions. That's why solving these issues typically results in a seemingly endless series of illustration 'do-overs' and additional meetings that create WOE—delaying decisions and killing sales—making the complex sales process more difficult for both customers and salespeople.

As problems and decisions increase in complexity, the rules of selling change. The following list suggests some of the rules (or laws) that result.

The Laws of Complex Selling

When it comes to selling, *the more complex a problem is:*

(1) *The greater the value you create for clients.* Complex problems aren't bad. They're real. Life isn't simple—it's complex. If life's problems were simple, clients wouldn't need you. *Salespeople add the most value in assisting customers with hyper-complex problems.*

(2) *The more what-if questions will take place.* There is a direct relationship between the level of complexity and what-if questions clients ask. That's because there are usually more things that can go right and wrong...and the relationships between what you do and what you get are not as clear.

(3) *The less value you get from static tools.* Pictures and printouts are static...they are typically set in ink. The client's understanding of the issues is not. It evolves. As soon as clients understand the issues, they're likely to start asking you new questions and/or providing you new information.

(4) *The less value you get from modular tools (tools that break the problem into pieces).* You can't break complex problems into pieces because of the interdependent nature of the issues involved. You need a set of binoculars, not a microscope.

(5) *The more likely that people will react on emotion not logic.* When people are faced with complex problems, the most common responses are for them to: freeze and do nothing; react impulsively and do anything; or simply revert to patterns of behavior that have worked for them before.

(6) *The greater the emphasis on trust in the decision and sales process.* When it comes to

providing advice on complex problems your options are '*Show Me*' or '*Trust Me*'. If you can't show people, the level of trust required for them to move to action goes up significantly. The inability of most salespeople to be able to show customers the answer to complex questions and having to revert to 'trust me' selling is one of the leading reasons why most customers and many salespeople consider the practice of selling manipulative.

(7) *The longer the sales cycle and the lower the likelihood of closing a sale.* As complexity increases so typically do sales cycles. That's because greater complexity usually means more questions, more options, and more meetings…increasing the likelihood that the prospect or client will get stuck in the 'no-decision zone'.

Complexity and Sales Objections

Sales objections are client introduced delays in the sales process; concerns and questions that the customer may have about the proposed solution.

Salespeople are traditionally trained to manage or overcome objections by avoiding, eliminating, or minimizing these obstacles to keep the sale on track. They are taught that the problem is lack of thoroughness. "You didn't complete the prior steps, so that's why you had to revisit them." This leads to the view that sales objections are the result of a deficiency in interviewing ability or applying improper techniques.

This illustrates a fundamental misunderstanding of the real problem. 'What if' questions are a type of 'objection' that are a natural part of solving complex problems. In fact, as complexity goes up, so do customer 'what-ifs'. These questions demonstrate regression—a natural (and desirable) part of the learning cycle. Complex problem resolution and decision-making can't occur without them. Trying to overcome, control, or manage them gets in the way of complex decision-making by slowing it down.

Attempts to control objections create more objections and decrease trust. That's why customers tend to see salespeople as pushy. When you're trying to solve complex problems, tradeoffs are inevitable. Changes are inevitable. They are not something to be avoided or objections to be overcome.

Complexity is not the problem. The fact is that salespeople have to 'overcome' objections when they don't have the capability (tools, methods, and training) that allow them to explore and solve them. A different way of looking at, thinking about, and addressing these problems is needed. Fortunately, there is a growing body of work in this area to support our efforts. Researchers in the physical sciences, psychology, and other areas have made significant contributions to the development of theory, methods, and tools for managing complexity.

In the next chapter, we provide an overview of three topics that have resulted from this work: Systems Thinking; Simulation; and Scenario Planning. We'll describe their relationship to each other and how they address the sales challenges posed by complex problems.

8

MANAGING COMPLEXITY

"What is the right decision? It varies from case to case, but there is one common element to all correct decisions. They include a consideration of the bigger picture."
—Peter Schwartz

In the last chapter, we talked about complexity—what it is and some of the challenges it creates for problem solving, decision making, and selling.

This section describes *Systems Thinking*, *Simulation*, and *Scenario Planning*: three fields that have emerged from management, mathematics, and psychology sciences to help understand how complex systems work and how to more effectively manage complex problems.

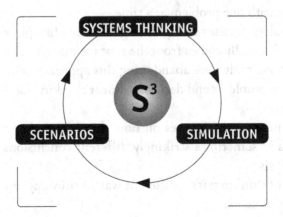

We're not going to try to cover these subjects in-depth here—but simply provide a foundation for the concepts we'll build on in subsequent chapters.

Systems Thinking

What Is Systems Thinking?

Systems Thinking [8.1] is based on Systems Dynamics, a field introduced over 40 years ago by Jay Forrester at MIT.

Systems Thinking is a language used to model the behavior of complex systems that makes them easier to understand, explain, and interact with.

Examples of situations where Systems Thinking has proven its value include problems:
- Involving people or groups with different opinions and agendas
- Having been made worse by past attempts to fix them
- Having a significant difference between the short-term and long-term benefits
- Having either no right answer or the solutions are not obvious

A Different Way of Thinking

When we're struggling with problems, we tend to use *Linear Thinking* to simplify things, to create order, and to work with one problem at a time.

Traditional linear analysis focuses on separating the individual pieces of what is being studied; in fact, the word 'analysis' actually comes from the root meaning 'to break into constituent parts.'

Systems Thinking doesn't advocate abandoning this approach completely. Instead it reminds us that for certain types of problems and decisions, linear thinking has limits, and can generate as many problems as it solves.

Systems Thinking, in contrast, focuses on how the thing being studied interacts with the other parts. This results in sometimes strikingly different conclusions than those generated by traditional forms of analysis.

It's not a better way of thinking; it's a different way of thinking; and a more appropriate way of thinking for complex problems.

Principles of Systems Thinking

In general, systems thinking is characterized by these principles:
+ Balancing short-term and long-term perspectives
+ Thinking of the big picture
+ Recognizing that systems aren't linear
+ Taking into account both quantitative and qualitative factors
+ Using models that are visual, not verbal

Balancing Short Term and Long Term

How do you balance the short term and the long term? What works today might not seem like such a good idea tomorrow. An example in business would be laying off customer service people to improve profits. It saves money today and could hurt you in the future.

In thinking about any decision, the best approach is to strike a balance, to consider short-term and long-term options and to look for the course of action that encompasses both.

Systems Thinking provides a way of looking at issues that provides a clearer connection between the short term and the long term to strike an appropriate balance.

The Big Picture

Every problem or decision you face is part of a larger issue. When you look at the world from a big picture perspective, it's apparent that everything is connected and that everything we do has some impact, at least potentially, on everything else.

To discover the source of a problem, you have to widen your focus to include that bigger system. With this wider perspective, you're more likely to find a more effective solution.

Systems Thinking emphasizes looking at larger wholes rather than smaller parts.

Systems Aren't Linear

Cause and effect relationships in simple problems are direct and clear.

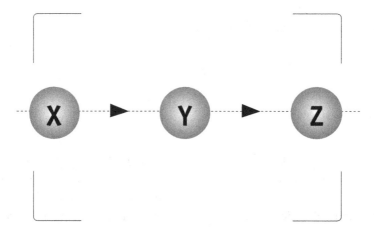

In complex problems, they are indirect and unclear. Systems Thinking is a circular rather than linear language. In other words, it helps describe how X influences Y; Y influences Z; and Z comes back around to influence X.

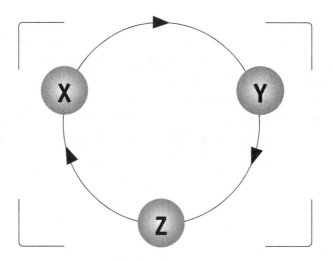

Quantitative and Qualitative Data

Systems Thinking encourages the use of both quantitative and qualitative data, from measurable information such as sales figures and costs to harder to quantify information like morale and customer attitudes. Neither kind of data is better; both are considered important. Systems Thinking promotes *double-loop accounting*: understanding the stories that back up the numbers.

MODEL: rules, equations, and/or constraints for generating behavior resembling that of a system; physical, mathematical, or logical representation of a system, entity, phenomenon, or process.

Visual Models

"I understand it. But I can't explain it." One of the reasons people have difficulty communicating complex ideas is they might be using the same words while picturing the problem differently.

Complex issues are much easier to grasp and communicate when people can 'see them.' Systems language uses visual tools, including causal loop diagrams and BOT (behavior over time) graphs, to create visual models of complex problems.

Models not only help us look at problems—they are powerful tools for helping people talk about them. They help make sure everyone is looking at the same problem. They allow us to see and challenge our thinking.

As a result, they are useful to help improve communications on the conflicting issues and tradeoffs that naturally occur when resolving complex issues.

The Connection Between Systems Thinking and Simulation

A systems model is the representation of a process. It illustrates how parts of a system interact.

These models can range from very simple to highly complex depending on the characteristics of the object or process they represent.

Even drawing relatively modest models can be challenging to create because the number of possible interactions increases dramatically with each new variable considered.

How do you deal with the number of issues and possible outcomes associated with more complex models?

One solution is the use of computer simulation.

Simulation

"If you want truly to understand something, try to change it."—Kurt Lewin

What Is Simulation?

Simulation [8.2] is a process that involves evaluating the behavior of a model by introducing changes. Properly designed computer-based simulation models can demonstrate the results of very complex systems quickly and effectively.

Why Is It Important?

When you create a model or a map of a system, you have done nothing more than propose hypotheses—ideas on paper. These hypotheses require testing.

Simulation provides a powerful way for people to test ideas and gain practical experience when real-life experience is impractical or too costly.

Intuition helps us guess what might happen. It helps us 'jump to conclusions', which sometimes work. But people's intuition about complex problems is usually flawed, because complexity is counter-intuitive. Like backing up a car pulling a boat or a trailer, you feel like you should be turning left, when you should really be turning right.

Computer models can help us see what happens when we play things out. They provide new and less risky ways to test ideas before we act on them. They help us experiment with the results of our decisions.

Flight simulators provide a good example. You don't get too many chances of landing a plane wrong. Flight simulators have proved very useful in training pilots, reducing accidents, and saving lives. Likewise, other types of business and decision simulators can help people learn, improve results, and avoid costly errors.

Without modeling, we might think we are learning to think holistically when we are actually learning to jump to conclusions. A well-crafted and well-tested simulator gives valuable feedback by showing us the implications of our decisions that help us understand and handle big picture issues more effectively.

The Connection Between Simulation and Scenario Planning

Computer simulation provides a very powerful way to evaluate the possible outcomes of decisions. But there are two potential dangers:

- Design Flaws
- Inappropriate Use

Design Flaws

Simulation models are very effective at modeling how well defined processes work. The usefulness of the models is limited by the skill of the designer.

For example, no one denies that spreadsheets are useful. But they also lowered the technical barriers facing people who wanted to do financial modeling. As a result, in the first few years after the introduction of spreadsheets, the average quality of financial models plummeted. Today, many financial models are not only useless, but downright harmful to decision-makers who use them to justify poor decisions.

Inappropriate Use

Let's suppose you have a computer simulation model…What shouldn't you do with it? Attempt to make predictions about the future!

Until about 10 years ago, there were various approaches used in anticipating the future, from computer-based mathematical forecasting models to Delphi surveys. All of them were attempts to predict, all of them were scientifically rigorous, and all of them failed because the future is unpredictable.

It is simply not possible to predict the future with certainty.

Appropriate Use

You can't *predict* the future but you can *prepare* for it. That's why scenario planning has won out as the accepted methodology in future studies.

Are you trying to predict the past or the future? Without scenario planning, simulation is a power tool to predict possible pasts (what we could have done). You need scenario planning to consider possible futures.

When you combine simulation tools with scenario planning methods, you have a powerful combination that can be used to help people plan more effectively for the future.

Scenario Planning

"He who predicts the future lies even if he tells the truth."—Arab Proverb

What Are Scenarios?

Scenarios [8.3] are stories about the future that help people prepare for what could happen...stories about the way the world might turn out tomorrow...stories that can help us recognize and adapt to changing aspects of our present environment. Scenarios provide a meaningful container to make sure data and information are understood and used appropriately. They provide a context for informational content to make it personally relevant and purposeful.

What Is Scenario Planning?

Scenario Planning is a method for articulating the different possible futures that might exist for you, and considering your appropriate movements down each of those possible paths. Scenario planning provides a way for people to rehearse the future, and to recognize opportunities and potential problems unfolding so they can act effectively and adapt appropriately.

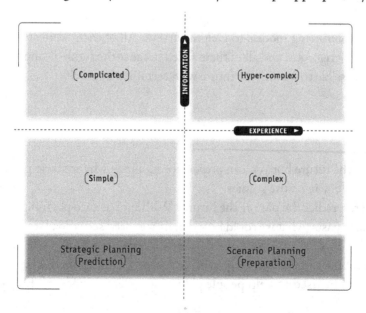

Unlike traditional business forecasting or market research, scenario planning presents alternative images of the future; they do not simply extrapolate the trends of the past or present.

The objective isn't prediction, but preparation. Scenario planning is a process to help people learn about possible futures to make better decisions today.

Scenarios and Learning

Learning is of particular importance for successful adaptation to an environment that is changing rapidly. Since that is exactly what people face in the 21st Century, a learning approach for problem solving and decision making is increasingly valued and necessary.

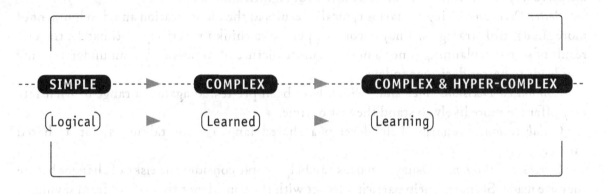

SIMPLE ----▶---- COMPLEX ----▶---- COMPLEX & HYPER-COMPLEX

(Logical) ▶ (Learned) ▶ (Learning)

How does a scenario planning process promote learning?

Creating Awareness: Scenarios engage people in discussion of their current situation as well as their desires for the future. This thinking helps the person by: heightening awareness of the need for change; and picturing a wider range of possible options and strategies.

Stimulating Creativity: Scenarios encourage people to stretch beyond traditional approaches for solving problems, and for thinking about possibilities.

Improving Discovery and Questions: Good scenarios cause people to consider the implications of their decisions. As a result, they ask better questions and deeper more meaningful discovery is accomplished.

Challenging Assumptions: To operate in an uncertain world, people need to be able to question their assumptions about the way the world works, so that they can see the world more clearly. Thinking through possible scenarios brings each person's unspoken assumptions about the future to the surface.

Exploring Opportunities: Scenarios help people identify surprises in all areas of their lives and understand these changes from different perspectives. They can also help determine which opportunities may provide the best outcome.

Reducing Risk: Scenarios help identify unseen or future challenges as well as opportunities. In addition, by recognizing the warning signals and the future that is unfolding, people can minimize the surprises, respond, and act effectively.

Overcoming Internal Obstacles: How do you judge whether learning takes place? Learning changes thinking and almost always changes behavior. A good scenario asks people to suspend their disbelief in its stories long enough to appreciate their impact. You know that a scenario is effective when someone, pondering an issue that has been taboo or unthinkable before says, "Yes. I can see how that might happen. And what I might do as a result." This power to break old stereotypes provides great opportunities for significant change.

Better Decisions: Using scenarios typically results in the identification and development of more thoughtful strategies. They encourage people to think proactively. Ultimately, the end result of scenario planning is not a more accurate picture of tomorrow but an understanding that leads to better decisions today.

Committed Decisions: Decisions which have been pre-tested against a range of what fate may offer are more likely to stand the test of time.

Collaboration: Scenarios help develop a shared language for talking about a shared future.

Increased Confidence: Using scenarios can help people consider the risks of changes before they are made. Scenarios help participants act with the confidence that comes from saying, "I have an understanding of how the world might change, I know how to recognize it when it is changing, and if it changes, I know what to do."

S³ – A Scientific Approach to Managing Complexity

You can't avoid dealing with complexity. The real world is complex, not simple. Intuition and logic alone can get us into trouble when dealing with complexity. So how do we handle them and make good decisions? To accurately describe and solve problems in an increasingly complex world, we need a new language with skills and tools to support it.

Systems Thinking, Scenario Planning, and Simulation provide us with the theory, methods, and tools we need to understand and manage complexity:

- Systems Thinking provides us with a language that makes understanding complex problems possible
- Simulation makes evaluating highly complex (real-world) systems models practical
- Scenario planning makes simulation purposeful for considering the future

Together, they provide an extremely effective way to understand, evaluate, communicate, and resolve complex problems.

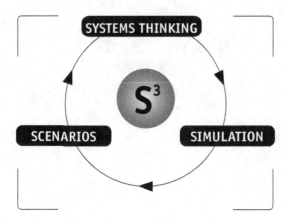

The next chapter brings us back into the realm of selling. We consider different selling methods and how they match up with the problem types we've identified. Then we begin to apply the theory, methods, and tools of managing complexity to selling.

THE ROLE OF HUMAN HELPERS IN PROBLEM SOLVING

"Systemic structure is often invisible until someone points it out."
—Chris Argyris [9.1]

In the last chapter, Managing Complexity, we saw that when solving certain types of problems (highly complex problems), technology is not only beneficial, it's necessary.

This raises a very interesting and important question...Technology may be necessary for solving complex problems, but are *other people* a necessary part of the problem-solving process?

There are many examples of where technology has already replaced a human helper in problem solving/selling processes.

If people can solve problems with technology but without other people, then it makes sense that sales technologies can be developed to eliminate salespeople from the process.

Is it reasonable to assume that technological innovations alone can eliminate the need for a human helper in all types of problem-solving/sales situations?

In this chapter, what we're going to demonstrate is...
- There are different types of helper roles
- There is no one best helper role or model
- Different helper roles are appropriate for different types of problems
- Which helper roles are difficult to replace with technology alone

Let's start by considering the options.

★ Four Possible Tech-Human Scenarios

If you're trying to solve a problem and you can involve a computer, another person (a helper), or both in the process…what are the possible combinations?

There are four possible ways you can interact with another person and/or technology.

#1. Technology & No Human Helper: You could use technology without another person (helper) involved in the process.

#2. A Helper Who Uses Technology for You: You could work with a helper who interacts with technology on your behalf.

#3. A Helper Without the Use of Technology: You could interact with another person without technology involved.

#4. The Helper & Technology Together: You could interact with a helper and with technology at the same time.

Why are we doing this? As you'll see, bringing technology into the discussion helps us:

• Describe and clarify the possible helper roles a person could play
• Determine which of them could be replaced by technology alone

Now, let's take a closer look at the different roles that the human helper plays in each of these scenarios. Each of the four scenarios/pictures we described suggests different helping models (and helper roles).

#1. Technology and No Human Helper (Self-Help Model)

The picture below illustrates a Self-Help Model. The client interacts with technology to analyze the problem or seek out solutions on their own without a helper.

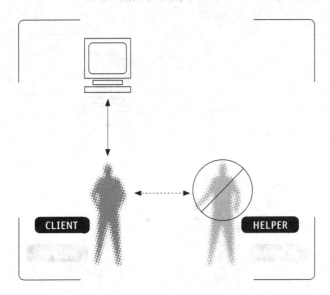

There are many problems where, given the right tools, you don't need another person involved. You can do it yourself. For example, most people don't need another person to help them use an ATM machine, surf the Internet, or execute a stock trade. The tool alone is sufficient.

#2. A Helper Who Uses Technology For You (The Consultant Model)

In some problem situations, you may need access to resources and knowledge beyond your reach and expertise. The helper role is a consultant/expert who uses their resources and knowledge to help the client solve a problem. This is the ***Consultant Model.***

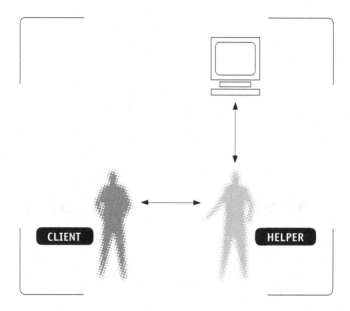

As the picture illustrates, the helper, not the client, interacts with the technology. Consider, for example, someone who uses tools to analyze data and prepare recommendations for the client. The consultant works on the problem for them.

#3. A Helper Without the Use of Technology (The Counselor Model)

In other types of problems, you may be able to solve the problem yourself, but doing so requires objective feedback and guidance through the process. This suggests a *Counselor Model.* [9.2] As the picture below illustrates, technology is not a required part of the counseling interaction.

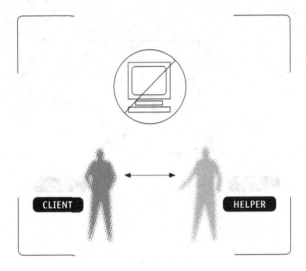

The helper's role is a facilitator who works with a client to resolve an issue by helping them talk it out: providing feedback, encouragement, and challenging the person's thinking. In other words, the helper is a human mirror providing a clear picture of the person's situation.

#4. The Helper and Technology Together (The Collaborator Model)

Some particularly difficult types of problems require clients and helpers to work together. This is a **Collaborator Model.** [9.3]

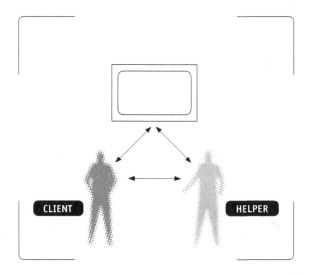

In a collaborative approach, the client and the helper interact with technology together. The client and the helper work as partners in separate but supporting roles to identify and resolve the issues.

Consultants...Counselors...Collaborators...

Are the differences in these roles simply a matter of semantics or real substance? One of the major challenges in separating these models is that people confuse the terms.

In summary, the differences are:

- Self-Help—I help myself
- Consultant—You help me by doing it for me
- Counselor—You help me help myself
- Collaborator—We do it together

Let's take a look at a model from educational psychology that helps further explain the differences between these roles.

★ Helper Roles Compared

Each of the comparisons in this section contrast two of the terms:

- Consultant vs. Counselor
- Counselor vs. Collaborator
- Consultant vs. Collaborator

Consultant vs. Counselor

What's the difference between a *consultant* and a *counselor*? More than just titles, they represent two distinctly different schools of thought and practice in the fields of training, education, and psychology. Consider the differences between *teacher-centered* and *learner-centered* instruction.

Direct Instruction: A Teacher-Centered Approach. Historically, the field of education has been oriented to models of learning that focus on classroom instruction. Most of the activity in the classroom has involved the teacher speaking and the student listening. The term 'teacher' has implied an expert who has information transmits it to students. Students are *empty vessels* who have information poured into them as they are 'taught'.

Constructivism: A Learner-Centered Approach. In contrast, a constructivist or learner-centered approach suggests that students learn better when they can invent knowledge through inquiry and experimentation instead of acquiring facts presented by a teacher in class.

At the risk of oversimplifying, the central difference between these two models is the order of study (information) and application (experience) involved in the learning process. As the picture below illustrates, a teacher-centered approach puts study before application; a learner-centered approach introduces application before detailed study.

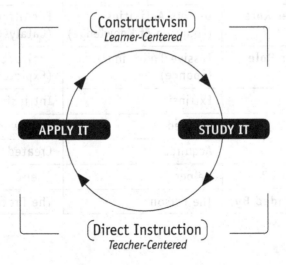

Constructivist lessons face students with a question that serves as a focus for the lesson. Students become problem solvers...going about analyzing and answering questions and taking greater responsibility for their own learning. Social interaction is encouraged to help students verbalize their thinking and refine their understandings by comparing them with those of others. Another way to describe it is radar learning—you learn by interacting with something and gain greater understanding as your ideas and experiences bounce off of it.

It's important to understand this difference because the roles (both teacher and learner) and methods each suggests are significantly different.

Table: Consultant vs. Counselor Approach

The table below outlines these differences.

	CONSULTANT APPROACH	COUNSELOR APPROACH
Educational Parallel	Directed Instruction (Teacher Centered)	Constructivism (Learning Centered)
Learning Process	Classroom Learning (Helper Explanation)	Discovery Learning (Client Exploration)
Model	Education (Builds on Logic)	Learning (Builds on Experiences)
Focus On	Outcomes	Process
Helper/Teacher Role	Directs Activities (Fountain of Knowledge)	Facilitates Activities (Catalyst/Facilitator)
Client/Learner Role	Passive/Following (Sponge)	Active/Leading (Explorer)
Motivation	Extrinsic	Intrinsic
Ability	Enabled	Empowered
Knowledge	Acquired	Created
Who's in Control?	Helper	Client
Structure Provided By	The Person	The Process

Although the constructivist-counselor approach appears less planned (to the outside observer), it requires more planning (and greater training) to be used effectively.

When using a constructivist approach, it feels like you have less control. Using it effectively requires a strong understanding and confidence in the process. You can't 'wing it'.

As a result of these misunderstandings: people often make the mistake of believing that they are facilitating a process when they are actually directing it; the untrained or inexperienced facilitator can easily slip back into directing mode to regain the feel of control.

When Is Each Appropriate?

Each model has its own strengths and weaknesses that make it more (or less) appropriate and effective depending on the types of problems being solved.

Direct Instruction is more appropriate when specific content and skills are the teacher's primary goals. For example: When working on basic skills and drills, or when dealing with absolute concepts and problems where there is only one correct answer. Direct instruction may also be more appropriate when a class is not ready to handle an activity or you're working with learners who need a lot of guidance.

Constructivism lends itself to higher order thinking and cooperative learning strategies. For example: Constructive teaching is good for science and math concepts so that learners can visualize and deduce on their own. It is also more appropriate when dealing with problems where there is no clear answer. Many abstract ideas can be made more realistic by embedding them in authentic tasks. The idea is that the experience makes the information more relevant and the learning more meaningful.

It is also important to realize that shifting from teacher-centered to learner-centered education does not suggest the teacher is suddenly playing a less important role. A teacher is equally critical and valued in the learner centered context, and is essential for creating and structuring the learning experience.

Counselor vs. Collaborator

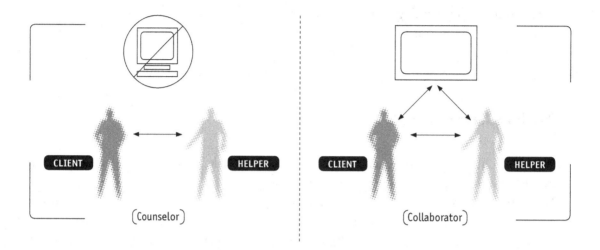

How is a counselor different than a collaborator? There are certain similarities:
* Both involve working together with a helper.
* Both are learning approaches.

The difference is in the use of tools for facilitation.
* The counselor model provides one feedback system: the helper (the human mirror).
* The collaborator model provides two feedback systems: a human mirror and a technological mirror.

The technological mirror creates a shared space: a prerequisite for effective collaboration. According to MIT's Michael Schrage, "All collaboration, without exception, requires shared space. If you're not using a shared space, you're not collaborating because it takes shared space to create shared understanding. You need to have media where ideas can be captured and represented and those representations can be modified and played with. Building models, mock-ups, prototypes, etc., together—either within the shared space or as the shared space—is at the heart of creative collaboration." [9.4]

Consultant vs. Collaborator

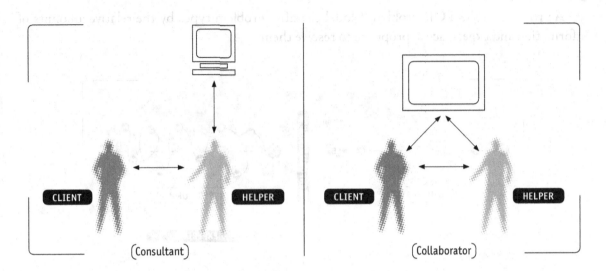

(Consultant)   (Collaborator)

What Is the Difference Between Consultative and Collaborative? Collaboration suggests a process of people working together to solve a problem, create something, or discover something. Consulting implies doing something for someone. Collaboration implies doing something with someone.

Self-Help, Consultant, Counselor, and *Collaborator...*Each of these models and the helper roles described *could be* applied to any type of problem. Where do they fit best?

Understanding the appropriate matches between helper-roles and problem types is critical to our discussion on selling. Why? Because it gets right to the heart of our questions about the purpose and the necessity of salespeople and the value they create. When there is a strong match between process and problem, greater value is created. When there is a weak match, less value is created because the problem solving process is less efficient and less effective.

What types of problem solving situations are each most appropriate for? Let's look again at our TOP Problem Model for suggestions.

⭐ ## Matching Problem Types and Helper Roles

As you recall, the TOP Problem Model classifies problem types by the relative amounts of information and experience appropriate to resolve them.

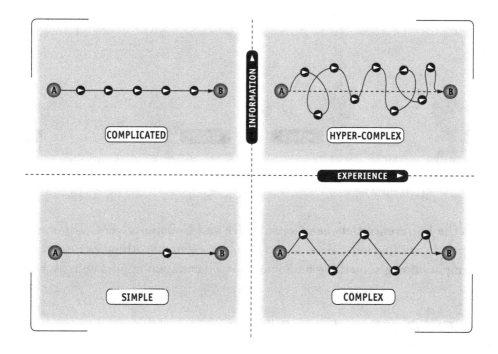

Simple and Complicated problems are linear/logical issues. Complex and Hyper-complex problems are non-linear/systems issues. These definitions provide us with a powerful clue to the value and role of helpers.

It's easier to build technological replacements for human helpers when the problem being solved is linear and logical.

One of the greatest challenges in systems problems is that it's difficult for the person to detach themselves from the issue they're evaluating. It makes it difficult to view their role objectively. One of the characteristics of systems problems is the need to put feedback systems in place.

Simple Problems → No Help Required

Simple problems require relatively little information or experience to resolve.

How do you resolve them? As we suggested in "How Do You Handle the Different Problem Types?" on page 114: When you're dealing with a simple problem, don't study it, sample it, or simulate it. *Just do it.* The *Self-Help Model* is an appropriate fit.

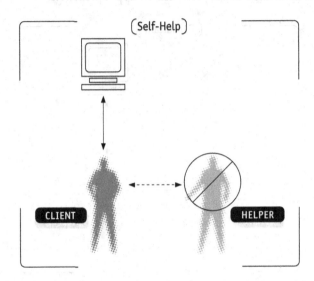

Can technology replace the role of the helper in Simple Problems? *Yes!*

Complicated Problems → Consultant

Solving complicated problems typically requires book smarts: greater information or education than required by simple problems.

How do you resolve complicated problems? Study them. Research them. Get out the manual. Complicated problems require a learn-ed approach. Either become an expert resource or go find one to help you. The **Consultant Model** provides an appropriate fit.

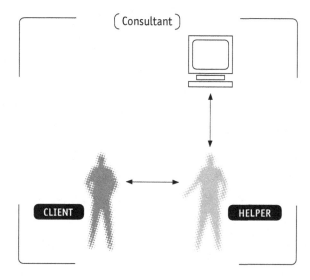

Can technology replace the role of the person in Complicated Problems? *Very Likely!*

Complex Problems → Counselor

As problems increase in complexity, so does the need for a human helper.

When dealing with complexity, information is less valuable and experience has greater value. So how do you solve complex problems? Sample. Experiment. Learn from your own experience or find someone who has 'been there and done that.' Complex problems require a learning approach. The **Counselor Model** provides an appropriate fit.

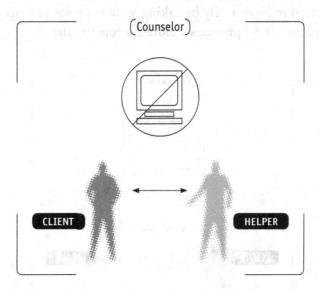

Can technology replace the role of the person in Complex Problems? Let's reframe the question…Can technology provide feedback and a learning experience without the participation of another person? *It's increasingly likely!*

As technology, especially computer software and multimedia tools, advances, it becomes easier to develop learning systems that don't require a human teacher in the process. Look at children's educational software, for example.

Hyper-complex Problems → Collaborator!

Hyper-complex problems represent a special class of highly complex problems that are difficult to solve without a high degree of information *and* experience.

There are many problems where it's not practical to learn from experience. These are life's hard lessons. They require both book smarts and street smarts. One or the other alone won't suffice.

When dealing with hyper-complexity, resolving problems typically results from vicarious experiences: learning from other people's experiences or finding some way to play out possible alternatives without actually going through them. Remember our example with the flight simulator...it's impractical to learn to fly by taking a plane up for practice or simply by reading about it. The Collaborative Model provides a more appropriate fit.

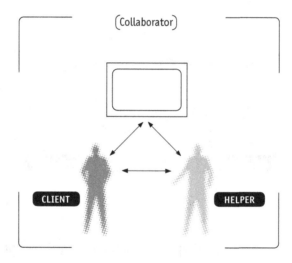

In the Collaborator Model, like the Counselor Model, the helper's role is a facilitator. But the helper also is an expert at interpreting feedback from the technology (i.e., reading the instruments).

Can technology replace the role of the person in Hyper-complex Problems? *It's very unlikely!!*

- It requires a great deal of work on the part of the client to get 'instrument rated'. Doing so changes the client's role. To eliminate the helper, they have to develop their skills.
- By changing seats, you eliminate the objectivity needed to deal with highly complex problems.
- By definition, collaboration requires more than one person. You can't collaborate with yourself!

Value Creation Requires a Proper Fit

In this chapter, we considered the role of other people, human helpers, in the problem solving process and addressed the question, "Are other people necessary?"

To help provide a framework for our discussion, we considered four possible human-tech scenarios involving different combinations of helpers and/or technology in the problem solving process. Each of the scenarios suggests a different role for the human helper which we titled: *Self-Help, Consultant, Counselor,* and *Collaborator.*

Each of these helper models and the processes they suggest *could be* applied to any type of problem. What types of problem solving situations are each most appropriate for? To help match up helper roles and problem types, we looked at how each role would fit into the TOP Model. Each type of problem defined by the TOP Model matches up with a specific helper role that provides a 'best fit'.

Understanding the appropriate matches between helper-roles and problem types is critical to our discussion on selling. Why? Because it gets right to the heart of our questions about the purpose and the necessity of salespeople and the value they create.

As problems increase in complexity…
so does the need for a human helper!

Hyper-complex problems (Type IV) are the only problem type that require two mirrors (a technological mirror and a human mirror). As a result, they are by definition the only problem types that require another person to be involved.

Matching Problem Types and Roles

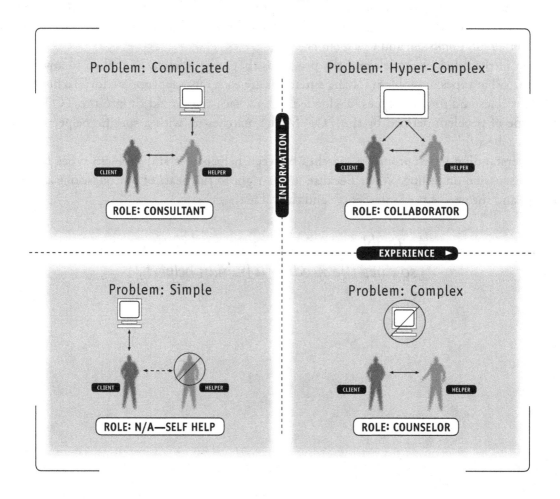

We'll cover the impact of problem types and helper roles on selling in more detail in the next two chapters. We'll show how different sales methods, seller roles, and technology-use match up with the problem types we've identified.

WHEN ARE SALESPEOPLE NECESSARY?

"For every complex problem, there is a solution that is concise, clear, simple, and wrong."
—H.L. Mencken

We spent the last few chapters talking about different problem types and effective ways to deal with them. In particular, we talked about the unique challenges and requirements of dealing with complex problems and how it differs from traditional analytic (linear) problem solving.

Why is this important for selling? Because it provides a framework that helps explain:
- Situations where salespeople can be replaced by technology.
- When salespeople are necessary.
- How they create the greatest value for clients.

In this chapter, we'll:
- Revisit the types of selling introduced in Part 1.
- See how they compare to the problem types and helping models we've identified.
- See how sales methods and roles are evolving to help address the increasingly complex problems people face.
- See how mismatches between sales problems and sales methods get in the way of selling.
- Consider what (if any) sales models and roles make salespeople irreplaceable.

Evolution of Sales Roles and Processes

Past and Present

In the History of Selling, we described the past (Transactional) and present (Consultative) sales models.

The role of the salesperson under transactional selling is as a pitchman or order taker for products and services. Transactional selling was and is a logical choice for a sales process to help customers when problems and solutions are simple and clear.

We saw how consultative selling evolved as a more appropriate and effective form to handle difficult problems. It upgraded the role and the image of the salesperson from a pitchman/order-taker to consultant-advisor in the process.

These two methods worked fine in an era of less change, choice, and uncertainty.

Neither method is appropriate or effective for dealing with problem types that have become increasingly prevalent in the Digital Age.

Sales Models/Roles: From Two to Four (Two New Roles Added)

As a result of increasing information and complexity, it's now more appropriate to segment the singular consultative 'expert' sales role into three more specialized roles that reflect the types of problems being solved. The chapter on "The Role of Human Helpers in Problem Solving" helps explain the new roles that result.

Each role requires different types of tools, and methods. As a result, *consultative selling* has really evolved into three different types of selling:

- Consultative Selling
- Counselor Selling
- Collaborative Selling

Different types of client sales problems and decisions require different types of selling approaches.

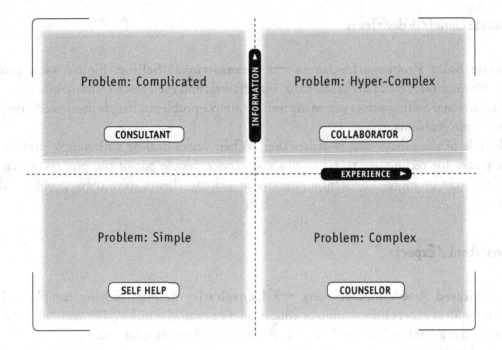

Just as different types of problems suggest different types of problem solving approaches...

What Can Technology Replace?

What does the model tell us about technology's ability to remove a helper/salesperson from the process?

Matching Sales Problems and Models

Let's see how these problem types match up with sales types and seller roles:
(1) Self-Help/Order-Taker (simple problems)
(2) The Consultative/Expert (complicated problems)
(3) The Counselor/Facilitator (complex problems)
(4) The Collaborative/Navigator (hyper-complex problems)

Transactional/Order-Taker

Simple Sales Problems/Decisions ⟶ **Transactional Selling.** Simple sales problems include, for example: retail purchases, bank withdrawals and even stock transactions.

Transactional Selling works extremely well for simple problems. People don't need salespeople to solve simple problems.

The role of the salesperson is order-taker. When you're dealing with simple problems, it's relatively easy for technology to take sales and service people out of the process. In fact, the technology may be more consistently effective at helping clients solve these problems than a person.

Consultant/Expert

Complicated Problems/Decisions ⟶ **Consultative Selling.** Solving complicated sales problems requires expert information or education. For example: picking between different types of stocks and mutual funds, or understanding how to read an insurance policy.

Complicated problems suggest a need for a trained technical expert. The technical expert/resource is valued for their education and the information they can provide. This is a match for the classical consultative 'salesperson as expert' approach.

Can technology replace the expert resource? It's already happening. If you need a question answered, why not 'Ask Jeeves' (www.askjeeves.com)? Expert resources and technologies available through the Internet have reduced the value of information to a commodity status. The introduction and advancement of technological *advice engines* illustrate the sophistication of new technologies for providing expertise. So, if you are being paid for what you know, chances are you can be replaced. Human browsers and search engines are more expensive and less efficient than their technological counterparts.

Counselor/Facilitator

Complex Problems/Decisions ⟶ **Counselor Selling.** Complex problems require expert experience.

The role of the salesperson as counselor is to facilitate customers through the problem-solving and decision-making processes.

Can technology replace the Counselor? Consider our metaphor of the counselor as a human mirror. Interview and assessment tools have proven to be more accurate and objective in some circumstances than people. The information gathered feeds heuristic (or learning) systems with the sophistication to help people teach themselves. Children's educational software and 'self-help' psychological programs provide good examples.

As a result, many lower level counseling/facilitating functions are capable of being replaced.

Collaborator/Navigator

Hyper-Complex Problems/Decisions ⟶ **Collaborative Selling.** Can technology replace the Navigator? Hyper-complex problems are especially difficult to solve without appropriate tools. But they are also difficult to solve without human involvement. For example, wealth planning (retirement & estate planning) is both complicated and complex. The advisor's skills and tools play a vital role in helping people navigate these issues.

Problem Type	Simple	Complicated	Complex	Hyper-Complex
Decision Type	Under Certainty	At Risk	Under Uncertainty	At Risk; Under Uncertainty
Old Methods	Transactional	Consultative		
New Methods	Transactional	Consultative	Counselor	Collaborative
Role	Order-Taker	Expert	Facilitator	Navigator

Dealing with Mismatches

Sales problem types and problem solver roles have evolved while the primary method to resolve them has stood still.

Mismatches are the result of applying the wrong method to a problem. It's a mismatch between the customer's concerns and the capabilities of the salesperson given the methods and tools that they are using. What happens when you have a mismatch? Let's look at a few examples.

Simple Problem + Consultative Process = SLOW

When you're dealing with a simple problem, a transactional approach works best. Don't waste your or the client's time talking about needs…take the order.

Complicated/Complex Problem + Transactional Process = PUSH

When you apply a transactional approach to a complicated or complex problem, the result is a 'push.' It results in an overly simplistic and canned approach that is inappropriate and unsatisfying.

Complex Problem + Consultative Process = WOE

As we showed in our chapter on Technology Disabled Consultative Selling, (Chapter 3) applying a consultative approach to a complex problem usually results in WOE…
+ Multiple meetings
+ And managing customer questions as sales distracting objections!

What's the real problem? Salespeople have to 'overcome' objections when they don't have the capability (tools and methods) that allow them to explore and solve them. 'What if' questions are a type of 'objection' that are a natural part of solving complex problems. In fact, as complexity goes up, so do customer 'what-ifs'.

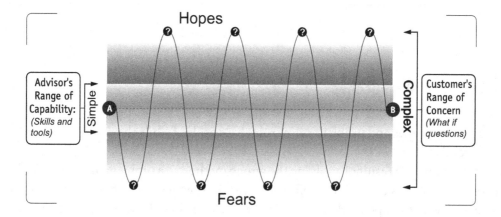

As complexity increases, so do 'what ifs'. The advisor's skills and tools play a vital role in helping people navigate these issues.

These questions demonstrate regression—a natural (and desirable) part of the learning cycle. Complex problem resolution and decision-making can't occur without regression and therefore can't avoid objections.

Trying to overcome, control, or manage objections gets in the way of complex decision-making rather than speeding it up. Why not embrace or even encourage objections instead? Salespeople have to 'overcome' objections when they don't have the capability (tools and methods) that allow them to explore and solve them.

How Can You Avoid Being Replaced?

In the past, selling was one of two basic types: transactional or consultative. Increased specialization is causing the two types to evolve into four types. Our TOP model helps explain the four new roles. Each type has its own methods and tools which can also be explained by our TOP model.

What can technology replace?

- Types I and II—Simple and Complicated problems—salespeople are easily replaced
- Type III—Complex problems—increasingly possible to replace salespeople
- Type IV—Hyper-complex problems—not likely to replace salespeople

If salespeople are going to survive, they must be able to help clients understand and solve complex and hyper-complex problems. Current sales methods and tools are not designed to do this. Most consultative salespeople apply the method they've learned like a one-process-solves-all approach.

But as the world and the problems people face become increasingly complex, these salespeople are challenged to justify their value because the tools and training that have worked in the past are ineffective at helping customers deal with the increasingly complex problems they face in the Digital Age.

In the final chapter of this section, *Technology & Selling Reconsidered*, we describe what's necessary to bridge the digital divide.

TECHNOLOGY & SELLING—
RECONSIDERED

"We need to shift away from the notion of technology managing information and towards the idea of technology as a medium of relationships." [11.1]
—Michael Schrage

High-Tech, High-Touch, or...?

When it comes to selling, are you *High Tech* or *High Touch?* Conventional wisdom suggests that it's an either/or proposition. But customers and salespeople in the Digital Age will inevitably interact with technology at some point in the buying/selling process, particularly when dealing with complex problems. So what can we do to use it to our (and our customer's) greatest benefit?

The early days of television help illustrate the problem—and the solution. Picture the anchor person, sitting behind a large desk, with a large microphone...*reading the news*. When TV was first invented, they showed radio! Why? They were using *new tools*, but they were applying *old thinking*. Of course, over time television's innovators added audiences, movement, color, and other features as they learned how to maximize the potential of the new medium.

Today this same scenario applies to professional selling. Widespread use of computers in selling has really only taken hold in the last 10 years. And during this time, advances in technology have dramatically outstripped our ability or understanding of what to do with them. Salespeople's new personal computers have horsepower capable of Hollywood quality media productions. What do most salespeople use them for? Computer printouts, emails, and simple PowerPoint type presentation slideshows. (New tools...but old thinking.) Like the transition from radio to television, these new sales technologies will <u>require</u> new methods to reach their potential.

In the next 10 years, salespeople will dramatically change the way they use technology to sell as they learn to adapt their methods to the medium. They must. Their survival in the Digital Age depends on it.

But how and what will it look like? The picture below describes two possible combinations of sales tools and processes, which we call: *Technology-Enabled Selling* and *Technology-Based Selling*.

It's important to note that these aren't additional sales processes; they are descriptions of different ways to integrate sales tools and methods.

⭐ Technology Enabled (or Disabled) Selling

Technology-Enabled Selling[11.2] (or TES) describes how most people today attempt to do High-Touch selling *with computers*.

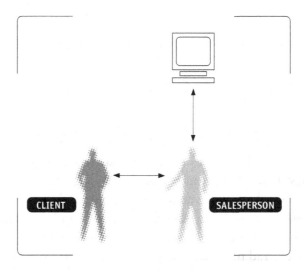

For many salespeople and companies, though, the result is Technology *Disabled* Selling—as they continue to apply old methods and ways of thinking to the new tools with frustrating results.

Let's take a look at the steps involved to see what happens in the typical technology-enabled consultative sales process.

- You meet to gather the information you need for analysis and illustrations.
- You leave the client to go do this work.
- You set up another meeting to show them what you did.
- You ask for the business. Problem solved. Sales closed. Right?

Here's the problem…This assumes that during your presentation, the client provides no new information and only asks questions that you've prepared illustrations for. But, if they do, you've got two choices: try explaining it away (reverting to 'trust me' selling); or going away to do it over…and over.

We described this unnatural phenomenon in Chapter Three as the 'Wizard of Oz Effect'—where the expert has to keep going behind the curtain. WOE usually results in a series of meetings that frustrate sales advisors and clients—delaying decisions and often killing sales.

There are a lot of good salespeople who avoid using technology or implementing a real consultative planning approach as a result. Companies struggle to reconcile the importance of planning, while realizing and hiding the fact that most of their best salespeople don't do it. In turn, this makes it harder to get other people to do it and build a 'consultative planning approach' into the culture. What you end up with is a consultative selling 'veneer', on a product/service selling core—planning in word but not in fact.

Consultative selling gurus and salespeople have developed a series of 'work-arounds' and apologist positions to deal with the multiple-meeting problem:

- Gathering as much information as you can up front so we have everything
- Spending a lot of time up front building trust (so people won't question advisor recommendations)
- Developing expertise in managing 'objections' in case they do
- And creating the image that taking a lot of time means we're doing a lot of work and creating a lot of value.

In reality, all of these multiple meeting myths are excuses that have been institutionalized as facts because we haven't had a way to quickly and efficiently address questions and integrate new information into already completed plans and presentations.

Why? Because when consultative selling was introduced in the 1960's, 'sales technologies' weren't an issue. For all practical purposes, they didn't exist. So, the consultative sales process didn't account for them and doesn't accommodate them. All current consultative selling programs are basically reworded versions of the early model. If you look at text books on consultative selling, there still aren't any of them that talk about how to integrate analysis and technology into the process.

But now that we live in an age where sales tools are ubiquitous—not only are they accepted, they are an expected part of most selling situations. So how do you keep from shuffling back and forth between separate interactions with a customer and a computer? Technology-*Based* Selling provides an answer.

Technology-Based Selling

Technology-Based Selling integrates technology into the sales process by design. For example, technologies typically used in the backroom (away from the client) are brought into the front room (in front of the client) so that clients and salespeople can use them together. This way, questions and new information can be entered quickly and new results can be seen immediately.

As a result, Technology-Based selling is *visual* and *interactive*. The technology shared between salesperson and prospect becomes a shared space. Why is this important? It mirrors the way that people naturally learn and make decisions. It meets necessary pre-conditions for people to *collaborate* effectively.

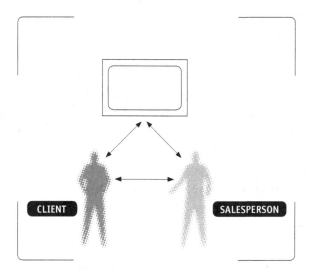

Technology-Based selling provides a way for us to achieve our desired objective of just-in-time selling because it holds the potential to play out alternatives and answer questions 'on-the-fly' rather than go away to prepare answers. This reduces the number of separate steps required for sales situations which require planning and analysis.

The potential benefits to this are great for both the client and the advisor, including a better customer experience and increased sales productivity.

So, is it as easy as turning around the computer and looking at the screen together during the sales process? No. As you'll see in Part IV—The Future of Selling, turning the screen around fundamentally changes how sales tools are both used and designed.

IV

THE FUTURE OF SELLING

Part IV

INTRODUCTION

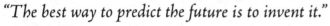

"The best way to predict the future is to invent it."
—Alan Kay

In Part IV of this book, we'll talk about selling's future.

We'll introduce a new model for professional selling that integrates sales tools and methods to pull the curtain on the 'Wizard of Oz' and eliminate the WOE that results.

FROM CONSULTATIVE
TO COLLABORATIVE

The simple act of turning the computer around for people to look at it together has profound implications. When you draw the curtain on the Wizard of Oz and involve prospects in all stages of the sales process, the process changes from *consultative to collaborative*.

The term collaboration [12.1] is currently a buzz word that is thrown around without most people having any idea of what it is or how to do it. Many people use the two terms, consultative and collaborative as if they mean the same thing. *Collaboration is a very different process than consultation.* Understanding the difference between these two terms is a critical 1st step in understanding how to design and implement the fast-professional sales model we're looking for.

What Is the Difference Between Consultative and Collaborative? Collaboration suggests a process of people working together to solve a problem, create something, or discover something. Consulting implies doing something FOR someone. Collaboration implies doing something WITH someone.

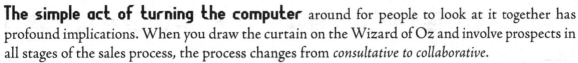

How Do You Collaborate?

The process of collaboration involves creating a shared space to play out ideas together and create a shared understanding. If you're simply having a conversation, you are not collaborating. All collaboration, without exception, requires shared space. It takes shared space to create shared understanding. What does a shared space look like? A blackboard or whiteboard can be a shared space. A flip chart, a piece of paper, or even a bar napkin can work as a shared space.

But when collaborating on highly complex problems, static models on paper have limited usefulness. You need to have media where ideas can be captured and represented and those representations can be modified and played with.

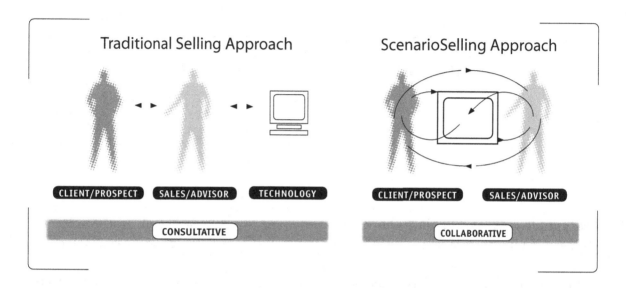

That is why computers, interactive software, and multimedia projectors are absolutely ideal. They can help create a theater-like collaborative sales experience.

Any Change, even a change for the better, is always accompanied by drawbacks and discomforts.
—Arnold Bennett

*Change Management isn't supposed to make people feel comfortable. It's supposed to help people deal with the natural **discomfort** that accompanies change.*
—Dr. David Lazenby

★ Characteristics of a Collaborative Sales Approach

The table and descriptions below describe some of the other differences between a consultative and a collaborative sales process.

	Consultative	Collaborative
Type of Planning	Goal-Based Strategic Planning	Possibility-Based Scenario Planning
Understanding	Logical	Emotional
Buyer's Role	Observing	Engaged
Seller's Role	Performing	Facilitating
Tool Design	Static/Inflexible (Difficult to illustrate changes)	Interactive (Designed to play out changes)
Conversation	Discussion	Dialogue
Solutions	Created for	Created with
Tasks	Organization; presentation	Exploration; discovery
Vision	Divisive: your view vs. my view	Cohesive: our view
Negotiation	Win/lose or compromise	Win/Win
Objections	Slow the process down	Speed the process up
Use of Technology	Presentation; Shared Information	Exploration; Shared Experience
View of Technology	Impersonal	Interpersonal

Type of Planning. Both consultative and collaborative selling are need-based approaches. But consultative assumes that people know what they want. Collaborative assumes they don't. You play out scenarios to determine what someone wants.

Understanding. Consultation is mono to collaboration's interactive 3-D. It's like the difference between watching a game and playing in one. Collaboration is a dramatically different and more powerful experience that grips hold of people's senses and involves them emotionally and not just logically.

Buyer/Seller Roles. When we move from a consultative to a collaborative sales process the buyer and seller roles change significantly. The buyer is no longer an observer, they are an active participant. For the buyer, it's the difference between buying a cake from someone and making a cake with them.

The seller's role changes from expert-performer to expert-facilitator.

Tool Design. Tools designed for consultative selling typically are designed for printouts or presentations. They are typically static—not designed to illustrate changes. Tools needed for collaboration must be dynamic by design. Collaboration involves playing out changes and scenarios and, therefore, values process over printouts.

Conversation. Collaboration shifts the role of spoken language from debate to discussion to dialogue. The listener's focus shifts from passive to active listening as ideas are played out in the shared space.

Interview. Consultative selling focuses on fact-finding. Collaborative selling focuses on discovery and exploration. Collaborative technologies promote information sharing. The new technology makes capturing, editing, and playing with fresh ideas relatively easy. Psychological research demonstrates that people will respond more openly and honestly to questions when they are being entered into a computer. Instead of simply being used to gather data, the interactive nature of the technology and process encourages the prospect to describe concerns and desires. Do-overs encourage exploration and discovery!

Solutions. Collaborative technologies create an engaging environment for joint problem resolution and value creation. Instead of solving problems FOR their clients, collaborative salespeople are now solving problems WITH their clients.

Vision. In the consultative model, the salesperson's expert role naturally results in a divide between the prospect and salesperson—each who has their own view. A collaborative process results in people creating a common perspective, or single view that they created together and share.

Negotiation. Collaboration changes the very nature of negotiation. When people have separate views, the best case negotiation typically ends in compromise. But when people are working with a common view towards a common goal, it increases the likelihood of win-win negotiations.

Commitment. Collaboration creates the highest form of buy-in. People have greater commitment to things they have created. It increases the likelihood that people will stick with their decisions.

Action. Collaboration results in greater accountability and action. Collaborative environments give people the incentive to produce something that can be displayed. It improves the likelihood that things that get planned will get done!

View of Objections. One fascinating result is that when you integrate the tools of analysis into the process, traditional sales objections become your friend. Clients and salespeople work together to pull in the same direction. As a result, shared understandings develop more quickly, accelerating trust and relationship building.

View of Technology. Collaborative tools completely transform use of computers in the sales process. When you use a computer in front of someone, it's not impersonal anymore—it's interpersonal. It doesn't just help them share information; it helps them share an experience.

The potential for an interactive multimedia approach exists in virtually every sales environment. This raises some very interesting questions:

- What happens to the traditional roles of salesperson and buyer in the new environment?
- Will customers come to insist on collaboration?
- Will salespeople be able to tailor their pitches and processes to take advantage of the technology?
- More explicitly, will salespeople be able to work collaboratively with their clients?
- Would they really be selling anymore or would they be performing another kind of service?

Clearly, turning a sales process into a technology-based collaborative exercise redefines the sales process and the very purpose of technology in that process.

The Benefits of Collaborative Selling

By integrating technology into the sales process to create a collaborative approach, a salesperson is able to:

- Change the sales process from a series of boring and painful meetings to an engaging and interesting session of interactive play
- Get more and better information…to improve the interview process
- Enable recovery from mistakes and wrong assumptions
- Shorten the sales cycle by eliminating unnecessary delays and meetings
- Capture and keep people's attention
- Let people try on solutions before they have to live them or buy them
- Develop trust faster
- Help people solve complex problems with a big picture approach
- Facilitate collaboration to get people on the same page; to help them work and make decisions together
- Help people buy rather than feeling like they're being sold

As a result, this process helps salespeople increase their sales productivity, differentiate themselves from competition, and clearly demonstrate the value they provide; while providing a dramatically better experience for the customer.

What's Required?

We described technology-based selling as visual, interactive, and collaborative. Achieving all three objectives requires us to redesign both the tools and the process of selling.

Consider the changes we're suggesting: Using the computer in front of someone; integrating analysis into the sales process; having the prospect participate in all stages of the sales process; and entering information and answering questions in real time.

Implementing these changes effectively requires:
- A different process (collaborative rather than consultative)
- Different tools (visual interactive tools designed to be used in front of a customer rather than away from the customer)
- And different skills (both technological and interpersonal).

So far we've used several very functional sounding names to describe this new process, including:
- Technology-based collaborative selling
- Just-In-Time professional selling, and
- Visual interactive selling

We decided to give it a simpler name—*ScenarioSelling*.

In the next five chapters, we describe the process, tools, and skills required.

A LEARNING APPROACH

"The road to wisdom? Well, it's plain and simple to express.
Err and err and err again, but less and less and less."
—Piet Hein, Danish inventor and poet

What does the name ScenarioSelling mean? The inspiration for the name came from an article, *Scenario Planning: Planning as Learning,* by Arie DeGeus, [13.1] a noted author and expert in the scenario planning field.

We feel it's appropriate because ScenarioSelling is a collaborative *learning* approach to selling based on scenario planning principles.

ScenarioSelling means 'Selling as Learning.'

ScenarioSelling = Selling as Learning

Learning describes a process that involves a change in someone's *mental model*—or the lens through which they see the world.

What does it mean to say 'selling as learning'? Learning...for whom?

For the Buyer and the Seller

For the Buyer. What's the relationship between buying and learning? People who are buying are making decisions. Decision-making is a learning process.

For the Seller. What's the relationship between selling and learning? (1) When selling, you're learning what the client wants and needs to move forward. (2) Where do salespeople really learn to sell? Most don't learn their skills in a classroom. They are gained and honed through experience in front of a client.

Buying/selling is a process that facilitates a learning relationship between buyers and sellers.

The Selling-Learning Relationship

A learning relationship is commonly defined as one that grows smarter with each interaction (Peppers and Rogers)[13.2]. As customers and salespeople explore problems, possibilities, and solution options, both learn more.

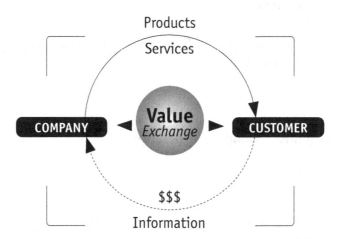

A collaborative learning approach to selling facilitates a learning relationship between the customer and the salesperson much more powerfully and effectively than a consultative 'teaching' approach.

The Learning Process

What do we mean by a learning approach and how is it different than an educational or teaching approach?

Education vs. Learning. Many people confuse the terms education and learning. What's the difference?

- Education is external and paced.
- Learning is internal and self-paced.
- Education is academic and intellectual.
- Learning is experiential and emotional.

It's important to distinguish between them because buying is the result of a learning process. Remember this important point. *You don't always have to use a learning approach in order to sell, but your prospects or clients must go through one before they'll buy.* What do we mean by learning process? Let's look at a model that helps explain it.

The Learning Wheel

The Learning Wheel [13.3] is a model that describes the process people go through as they learn. It implies that we learn by:

- Reflecting: Considering our situation (thoughts, feelings, and past actions)
- Connecting: Creating ideas and possibilities for action (generating hypotheses)
- Deciding: Settling on choices or methods for acting
- And Doing: Taking action (performing tasks)

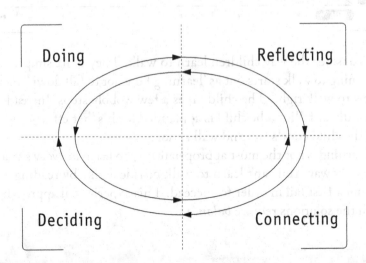

As the wheel illustrates, learning is a cyclical process. When you finish taking action, and consider "How well did it work out?", you immediately move back to the reflecting stage. The cycle repeats over and over as we learn and make adjustments to get closer to our desired results.

A Cyclical Ongoing Process

This process of 'cycling' is better represented by a series of loops, than a single circle (or a straight line). At the end of each cycle, there's a short step backwards (called regression) as people reflect and adjust to change.

The learning process continues with advances and regression—two steps forward, one step back—like the waves crashing on the ocean shore. They come up the beach, then go back. The next wave comes up a bit farther, and back again as, gradually, the tide rises.

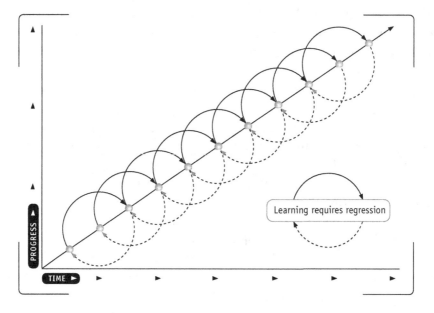

For example, consider the way children learn to walk. They don't simply get up one day and start walking. Learning to walk starts out as 'learning how not to fall down'. Parents don't provide instruction on how to walk right. The child takes a few wobbly steps. Instead of being chastised for walking awkwardly or falling, the child is applauded for his/her efforts and encouraged to try again. Gradually, the child crawls less and walks more.

Experiential learning is not the most appropriate way to learn in every situation, but for some situations, it's the only way. You can't learn to walk or ride a bike by reading a book. In many of life's lessons, you must first fail in order to succeed. This experiential approach is appropriate for problems in which the solutions require *balance.*

This concept fits our earlier description of complex problems. Complex problems are problems that involve balancing acts. If an experiential learning model is the appropriate approach for addressing complex problems, shouldn't our approach to complex selling be the same? Yes! Complex buying/selling situations suggest using a scenario-learning approach to selling.

Creating a Learning Model for Selling

How do we create a scenario-learning approach to selling? Let's take a look at the changes that take place as we transform the linear sales steps into a sales-learning cycle to create a sales learning model.

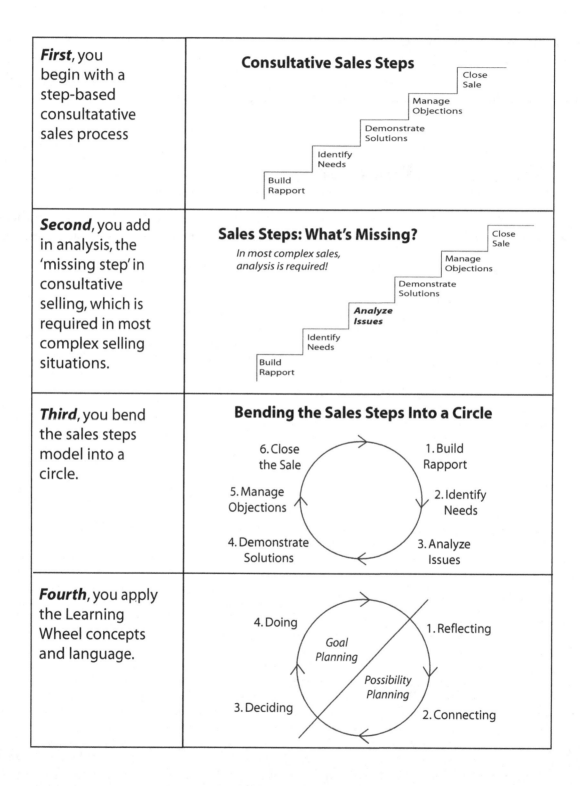

First, you begin with a step-based consultatative sales process	**Consultative Sales Steps** Close Sale Manage Objections Demonstrate Solutions Identify Needs Build Rapport
Second, you add in analysis, the 'missing step' in consultative selling, which is required in most complex selling situations.	**Sales Steps: What's Missing?** *In most complex sales, analysis is required!* Close Sale Manage Objections Demonstrate Solutions *Analyze Issues* Identify Needs Build Rapport
Third, you bend the sales steps model into a circle.	**Bending the Sales Steps Into a Circle** 6. Close the Sale 1. Build Rapport 5. Manage Objections 2. Identify Needs 4. Demonstrate Solutions 3. Analyze Issues
Fourth, you apply the Learning Wheel concepts and language.	4. Doing 1. Reflecting *Goal Planning* *Possibility Planning* 3. Deciding 2. Connecting

With these changes, the sales process starts to look like the way customers make decisions and purchases. The sales process starts to become customer-centered buying facilitation.

As you apply the Learning Wheel concepts and language:

- *Reflecting* (considering our situation—thoughts, feelings, and past actions) replaces the interview
- *Connecting* (creating ideas and possibilities for action—generating hypotheses) replaces analysis
- *Deciding* (settling on choices or methods for acting) replaces demonstration
- And *Doing* (taking action and performing tasks) replaces closing.

One of the challenges in using an experiential learning approach is that it can be slow. In the next section, we describe the conditions needed to accelerate the learning/selling process.

Accelerating Learning (and Selling)

"The ability to learn faster than your competitors may be the only sustainable competitive advantage in the future." —Jack Welch

One best practice model in the development of education and training for adults is *accelerated learning*. [13.4]

What is accelerated learning?

Accelerated Learning has been described as Whole Brain Learning, Integrative Learning, Quantum Learning and Holistic Learning. It describes methods and techniques to help people absorb and apply new information quickly.

Faster learning doesn't require us to hurry up. Faster learning requires simpler and more efficient ways to learn, fewer steps in the learning process, and more attention paid to applied (experiential) learning.

There are many books on the subject of accelerated learning. They include discussion of topics including learning styles, multiple intelligences, music, drama, visualization, and simulation.

It is not our purpose in this book to try to cover the entire field, but to provide an overview and demonstrate its relevance for selling and salespeople.

Why is accelerated learning important?

The world is changing at an ever-accelerating pace. Information is estimated to be doubling every four years and has already begun to overload people's attention capacity. In this environment, traditional teaching and training have reduced effectiveness and value. Interest in accelerated learning has grown because the ability to absorb and use new information quickly and effectively has become one of the most important skills a person can possess.

How do you accelerate learning? Let's take a look at a list of suggestions that we refer to as the 12 Principles of Accelerated Learning.

12 Guiding Principles of Accelerated Learning

1. *Accelerate learning through the use of different senses and media.* Learning is not all merely 'head' learning (conscious, rational, 'left-brained,' and verbal) but involves the whole body/ mind with all its emotions, senses, and receptors. (See additional information at the end of this section on learning styles.)
2. *Accelerate learning by actively engaging them in the learning process.* Learning is creation, not consumption. Knowledge is not something a learner absorbs, but something a learner creates. Learning happens when a learner integrates new knowledge into their mental model—a change in how they see the world.
3. *Accelerate learning through collaboration.* All good learning has a social base. We often learn more by interacting with peers than we learn by any other means.
4. *Accelerate learning by helping people see the big picture.* Learning is not a matter of absorbing one little thing at a time in linear fashion, but absorbing many things at once. The brain is a parallel processor that works to put pieces together. People learn best in context. Things learned in isolation are hard to remember and quick to evaporate.
5. *Accelerate learning by providing real and simulated experiences.* It has been said that on average we remember: 10 percent of what we read; 15 percent of what we hear; but 80 percent of what we experience. We learn how to swim by swimming, how to manage by managing, how to sing by singing and how to sell by selling. The real and the concrete are far better teachers than the hypothetical and the abstract provided there is time for feedback and reflection.
6. *Accelerate learning by providing entertaining experiences.* Learning is emotional. Feelings determine both the quality and quantity of one's learning. Negative feelings inhibit learning. Positive feelings greatly improve learning. Learning that is stressful, painful, and dreary fails. Learning that is fun, relaxed, and engaging works.

7. *Accelerate learning by providing visual explanations of information.* The brain absorbs image information instantly and automatically. The human nervous system is more of an image processor than a word processor. Concrete images are much easier to grasp and retain than are verbal abstractions. This is particularly true for complex information.

8. *Accelerate learning by taking people out of their comfort zone.* Traditional learning often attempts to make the learner 'comfortable' when, in fact, learning new things is inherently 'uncomfortable.' Accelerated learning attempts to provide an environment where people are OK feeling uncomfortable. Create an environment that promotes safe risk taking.

9. *Accelerate learning through the use of curiosity.* Research illustrates that the human brain loves surprises. As a result, it is drawn towards situations where outcomes are in doubt or something new is introduced.

10. *Accelerate learning through the use of personal relevance.* The adult brain is a finely tuned filter that blocks most attempts to capture its attention. Ideas that are of specific interest or relevance to individuals tend to get through more effectively.

11. *Accelerate learning by helping people see mistakes as shortcuts to faster learning.* Many people avoid mistakes at all costs; however mistakes are a key part of learning. You progress faster by making mistakes faster and avoiding making the same mistakes over and over.

12. *Accelerate learning by helping people clarify, test, and validate assumptions.* We all make many assumptions about the world we live in. Making assumptions allows us to be as effective. Assumptions fill in the blanks for things we don't or can't know. Imagine if every day we had to check that each part of the car worked before starting it. Unfortunately, incorrect and inappropriate assumptions can lead to very costly life lessons. The key to managing assumptions in the learning process is to make them explicit. Once they are 'out in public', you can test them to determine if the assumptions are valid.

Learning Styles

One of the keys to Accelerated Learning is the recognition that as individuals we all have preferred learning styles. In summary, these are:

- *Visual.* You prefer using pictures, images, and spatial understanding.
- *Aural.* You prefer using sound and music.
- *Verbal.* You prefer using words, both in speech and writing.
- *Physical.* You prefer using your body, hands and sense of touch.
- *Logical.* You prefer using logic, reasoning and systems.
- *Social.* You prefer to learn in groups or with other people.
- *Solitary.* You prefer to work alone and use self-study.

Using multiple learning styles and 'multiple intelligences' for learning is a relatively new approach. By ensuring that learning recognizes and utilizes these different styles, significant improvements in the speed and quality of your learning can be achieved.

How does this apply to selling?

Global consumers are pushing the world to change. This occurs because they demand better quality products and services. They want good service and they want it now. If one supplier is unable or unwilling to deliver what they want, they will simply go somewhere else.

Technology and business process innovations have resulted in speeding up all the components of the value chain: supply, manufacturing, marketing, distribution, and service. The final frontier of business productivity, effectiveness, and value creation involves helping customers make and implement buying decisions faster (just-in-time selling).

How do you accomplish this? If selling is learning, then we should be able to accelerate selling (problem-solving, decision-making, and action) through the use of accelerated learning principles. We suggest that the same principles that apply to accelerated learning must become the new standards for the sales process and experience.

The following list is a summary of the **12 Guiding Principles for Accelerated Selling** (*12 GPAS*) that results from replacing the word 'learning' with selling.

1. Accelerate selling through the use of different senses and media.
2. Accelerate selling by actively engaging people in the selling process.
3. Accelerate selling through collaboration.
4. Accelerate selling by helping people see the big picture.
5. Accelerate selling by providing real and simulated experiences.
6. Accelerate selling by providing entertaining experiences.
7. Accelerate selling by providing visual explanations of information.
8. Accelerate selling by taking people out of their comfort zone and creating an environment that promotes safe taking.
9. Accelerate selling through the use of curiosity.
10. Accelerate selling through the use of personal relevance.
11. Accelerate selling by helping people to understand that mistakes are just shortcuts that result in faster learning.
12. Accelerate selling by helping people clarify, test, and validate assumptions.

How many of these elements does your current sales process utilize right now? The fewer you use...the lower your sales GPA...the slower your sales process. The more you use...the higher your sales GPA...the faster you will solve problems and complete sales.

In the next chapter, we look at how this accelerated learning model helps speed up the sales process by accelerating the development of trust.

ACCELERATING TRUST

"Trust is speed."
—Peter Senge [14.1]

It is commonly understood and accepted that trust is vital to the sales relationship.

- For the client. Customers can make buying decisions most easily and confidently when they have trust.
- For the advisor. When trust is high, selling is easier. When trust is low, selling is harder.
- The Bottom Line. Trust is speed. When people trust each other, sales results are better and faster.

It's easy to see and understand the value of trust in the client-advisor relationship. But what is it and how can we create it? And how can we create it *faster*?

TRUST (n): Depth and assurance of feeling that is often based on inconclusive evidence. Assured resting of the mind on the integrity, veracity, justice, friendship, or other sound principle, of another person; confidence; reliance; reliance.

TRUST (v.):

1. To place confidence in; to rely on, to confide, or repose faith, in; as, we can not trust those who have deceived us.
2. To give credence to; to believe; to credit.
3. To hope confidently; to believe;
4. To show confidence in a person by intrusting (him) with something.
5. To commit, as to one's care; to entrust.
6. To give credit to; to sell to upon credit, or in confidence of future payment; as, merchants and manufacturers trust their customers annually with goods.
7. To risk; to venture confidently.

What Is Trust?

"I trust you." These are powerful words. But what do we really mean when we say we trust someone?

Feeling or Action

It's a feeling. For many people, the word trust means confidence. It's the peace of mind that comes when we know that someone has our best interests at heart. That's a description of the feeling. The feeling of trust is what most people mean when they discuss it. But trust is more than a feeling.

It's also an action! How do you show someone you trust them? You take chances. Trust implies risk. If you feel trust for someone, it implies a belief that they wouldn't cheat you or betray you. But the chance exists. That's why you must trust them.

So which comes first? The feeling of trust usually follows from the act of displaying trusting behavior. When people express themselves to others in a way that shows real caring, it is the action that results in caring, not the caring that results in action.

A Challenge: In Western society, we've become attached to the idea that people should trust us and love us without our taking responsibility to act in a way to help foster those feelings, or reciprocate them.

Trust and Comfort

Some people confuse building trust with making people feel comfortable. The feeling of trust involves comfort, but the act of trusting involves discomfort.

When asking people to take action, which comes first? In

selling, like in real life, the action of trusting usually precedes the feeling of trust. Many salespeople put the feeling before the action. They wait to ask people to act until they're convinced the people feel comfortable. This is a critical mistake that kills sales and keeps people from helping clients solve problems.

Selling is not about trying to get people to feel comfortable. It's about trying to help them feel ok about doing uncomfortable things.

Consider the steps taking place:

+ The less trust we feel, the more likely we are to try to take control.
+ Letting go of this control makes us feel uneasy.
+ Therefore, giving trust involves feeling uneasy.

You're going to feel uncomfortable first. Why? Because the act of trusting involves giving up control and taking risk!

Trust and Sales Pressure

For years we've heard terms like 'high pressure selling.' This usually referred to a salesperson who came on quite strong during the close or who tried to close too early and too often.

But, think a moment and see if you agree with this statement, "Selling pressure is a reality only when perceived so by the prospective client."

So what is pressure and how do prospective clients perceive it?

Where trust and rapport are high, decision-pressure and self-interest are usually perceived as low, regardless of how much there actually is.

But where trust and rapport are low, decision-pressure and self-interest are perceived as high, regardless of how much there actually is.

Now, stop and think about this for a moment. Understanding trust has everything to do with your success with helping people solve problems and make decisions underscores why trust and rapport impact selling so much.

Building Trust

Your Relationship Trust 'Account'

In <u>The Seven Habits of Highly Effective People</u>, [14.2] Steven Covey refers to relationship building like a bank account. In a relationship, there are positive interactions, which act as deposits, and negative interactions which act as withdrawals. If there are more positives than negatives, the relationship account grows. If there are more negatives than positives, the relationship eventually becomes bankrupt and ends.

The following table provides examples of things that build and tax trust. To build trust, you must find ways to make trust deposits and reduce unplanned trust withdrawals.

Your Trust 'Account'	
+ Increases	**– Decreases**
Expectations met	Expectations unmet
Solving Problems	Creating Problems
Good results	Poor results
Sincerity	Insincerity
Respect	Disrespect
Honesty	Dishonesty
Confidentiality	Lack of Confidentiality
Clients Best Interest	Your Best Interest
Adding Value	Reducing Value
Safe Environment	Unsafe Environment
Understanding First	Solutions First
Validation	Violation
A 'Trusted' Sales process	A 'Taxing' Sales Process
Quality Time	Wasted Time

For example: If you help people solve a problem, you make a deposit. If you create a problem for someone, you make a withdrawal.

Where Do We Start?

On Guard. One of the difficulties in selling is that you usually start out with a deficit. Most customers go into a sales situation with their guard up. The salesperson is seen as an adversary. They expect the salesperson to attempt to sell them something, so they show no vulnerability. This creates a difficult climate to help the customer make decisions and take action.

There are different starting points. You must realize not all people start in the same place. Some people start with trust. Some don't. Some are very trusting—they trust you until you violate it. Some are very untrusting—trust must be built from step one.

With some people you'll start out with a positive trust balance—it's yours to lose.

With other people you'll start out with a negative balance—you have to earn it.

Risk Taking

What is risk? In financial terms, risk measures the likelihood of getting what we expect. When risk is lower, it is more likely that our expectations will be met.

Trust is like risk. In relationships, trust increases based on our ability to meet or exceed people's expectations and decreases when we don't meet them. *Greater risk requires greater trust.* When clients are making complex decisions or difficult decisions, it's even a greater issue. Greater complexity requires greater trust.

Risk implies vulnerability. The act of trust is to make yourself vulnerable to someone. If someone tells you a secret or shares something they're not comfortable revealing, that's an example of showing trust.

Validating Trust. If you make yourself vulnerable to someone and they validate you, you get the feeling of trust.

Violating Trust. However, if you make yourself vulnerable to someone and they violate you, trust is withdrawn or 'taxed'.

One of the issues that results from having to earn trust is the illusion that trust takes time. In the next section, you'll see why this is not true and what you can do to help accelerate trust.

How Do You Accelerate Trust?

Conventional wisdom in selling suggests it takes a long time to build trust. The idea of trust taking time is a misunderstanding of cause and effect. **Because while time can help build trust—** *trust does not require time.*

To help understand this, let's look at how a psychologist is trained to create trust. A psychologist has professional training and experience in building trust quickly. They have to. They don't have the luxury of time to build the trust necessary to help people make significant changes.

If you want to build trust like a psychologist, think **ESP**:

◆ Environment
◆ Skills
◆ Process

Environment

You can't talk people into trusting you. You can't make people trust you. These are things you can't control. But you **can** create conditions that encourage the development of trust. This includes creating what psychologists call validating and safe environments.

A Validating Environment. A validating environment makes sure that there's a match between people's perceptions and what they see around them. (WYSIWYG—What You See Is What You Get).

For example: If you claim to be the most successful company in town, but your office or appearance does not reflect this, it creates a mismatch in the client's mind that taxes trust.

If you claim to be the most customer-centric company in your industry and every time the client calls you they get shunted to voice mail, the real message to the client is clear because *'what you do speaks so loudly, they cannot hear what you say.'*

Creating and maintaining a validating environment requires congruence between your words, your image, and your actions.

A Safe Environment. Every step in the ScenarioSelling process helps create a safe environment for the customer. From the time spent exploring the customer's life situation to the suggestion of advancing towards the next step, both customer and salesperson are taking risks and building trust in each other.

Building trust is not about making people feel comfortable. It's about creating an environment that allows them to be vulnerable and to take risks—to talk about their fears and concerns.

Skills

Are you trustworthy? As we have discussed, trustworthiness is based on many factors including:
- Reputation for honesty
- Ethics/Integrity
- Appearance of Sincerity
- Lack of motivation for personal gain

Trust requires more than good intentions. It requires skills including:
- Probing
- Empathy
- Attending
- Responsive Listening
- Summarizing
- And others

Most salespeople do these things, even when they don't recognize them in name. Trained people do them more effectively with better results. We cover the skills for building trust in greater depth in the chapter on Knowledge, Skills, and Tools Required (Chapter 16).

Process

Does your sales process build or tax trust? To get the answer, it's critical to understand the difference between trusting a person and trusting a process! It also requires us to re-evaluate how customers perceive us in our 'expert' role.

Why Does Trust Take Time for Most Salespeople?

Most traditional selling methods require trust to be built on the front end. They emphasize building **personal trust** up front by:
- Getting people to talk about themselves
- Asking them about things in their environment

The reason personal trust is emphasized is that the sales process is not trusted. The salesperson needs lots of deposits on the front end, because their sales process makes more withdrawals than deposits. They're asking a client to transfer money, give up money, or to make life-changing decisions. And they haven't taken the actions necessary to build up the trust bank account needed for the action to take place.

Trust is a function of risk. That's why salespeople are taught that it takes time to build trust in the sales situation. It's not that trust takes time, it's because you know the salesperson is in a position to stick it to you. It takes time to build confidence to the level that the client can feel OK about taking that risk.

Many types of consultative selling are thinly veiled attempts at making people feel better about buying products. There is an air of self-interest in the recommended answer. For example, how come when discussing financial issues with an insurance agent, it doesn't matter what the problem is—the answer always seems to be *more insurance*.

Do People Trust Experts?

Most sales methods pit customer and salesperson as adversaries in a take-no-prisoners show of strength. It's a battle of interests as the salesperson goes into hand-to-hand combat with the client and the salesperson pushes or tricks the client's wrist to the table! Where's the risk? All on the client's side, who just hopes that his shoulder won't be dislocated or his pockets picked clean.

It's different of course for advisors, *isn't it?* Advisors are 'expert' consultants, not pitch men. But even in this type of selling, trust is not a given. A consultative, "I'm the expert", approach simply isn't enough.

Trust must be earned and often the advisor's expert role gets in the way. Experts aren't vulnerable, and most people are trained to feel inadequate and inferior in an expert's presence.

Advisors taking risk? Earning trust requires the advisor to take risks too. Doesn't the idea of taking risks and potentially making mistakes fly in the face of the view of advisor as the 'expert'? Actually, making mistakes can improve a customer's confidence. They recognize that you're not perfect. It humanizes you. It allows people to take risks safely, and allows the advisor to take chances and become vulnerable. Both help accelerate trust.

Making mistakes is not the problem. It's the advisors ability or inability to recover from mistakes that cause the real problem. And, it makes the advisor more of an equal; one to be trusted rather than an all-knowing, expert sales adversary to be feared and avoided.

Recovery time. When someone asks a question, its better (if we can) to quickly validate the answer. When you have a suspicion of disbelief, time increases support for your suspicion. If you can't prove out or challenge your assumptions, they become valid—because we thought them.

Developing a Trusted Sales Process

Selling doesn't have to tax trust. It can accelerate trust if the entire process is constructed to create value and reinforce risk taking. Vulnerability must exist on both sides. Both salesperson and client must take risks. The process must be designed to make it safe to do so.

Safe risks accelerate trust. If you can accelerate safe risk taking, you can accelerate trust. For example: Most people are familiar with the 'fall and I'll catch you' team-building exercise. It takes trust to fall backwards, unsupported. If a teammate doesn't catch you, it could be painful…or at least embarrassing. It's OK for the person falling backwards to be nervous about it. They just have to be willing to fall and have faith they'll be caught. Their vulnerability and fear of falling then leads to trust.

Like other team building actions, falling back through space requires vulnerability, and the willingness to take a risk that is uncomfortable. But it is this risk that speeds the development of trust.

Vulnerability is often presented as a negative. Vulnerability can be productive. People don't have to like being vulnerable. They just have to accept and be open to it. In allowing someone to take risks safely, you've created an environment that helps accelerate the development of trust and as a result build their confidence.

If we can do it in management, why can't we do it in selling?

One Step Back…Two Steps Forward. Like parents helping a child learning to walk or ride a bike, relationships grow faster when you *limit regression*. You don't start by asking people to take large risk from which they may not recover. You start by asking them to take small risks, from which they can recover quickly. It's about making risk taking safe.

Humanizing the Expert. The advisor and the client get to know each other through the process. The advisor learns what issues are important to the client. The client learns about the advisor, too. This kind of vulnerability creates intimacy, which also enhances the development of trust. This creates tremendous value for advisors and for their clients.

A trusted sales method works more effectively for selling because it speeds and supports the development of trust. By following a trusted sales process with every step, you add to the balance of your trust relationship account. By the time we get to the stage at which the customer needs to make a buying decision, they are confident in the solutions proposed and decisions they make.

What does our accelerated learning sales model look like? As you'll see in the next chapter, when you apply scenario planning language to the learning model, the two worlds are merged and the transformation is complete.

THE SCENARIOSELLING MODEL

In this chapter, we'll introduce the ScenarioSelling model [15.1] and explain what's involved in facilitating the process.

The language and look of the ScenarioSelling model are similar to the Learning Wheel. The four parts of the model: *Discovery*, *Scenarios*, *Solutions*, and *Action* represent the stages clients and salespeople go through together during the client's learning, decision-making, and buying process.

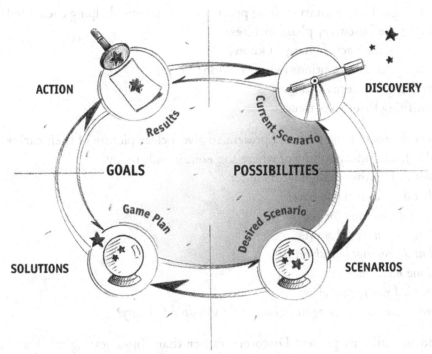

Discovery. Reflecting requires becoming an observer of one's own thoughts and actions. This can be done by examining one's prior experiences and behavior. In the Discovery stage of ScenarioSelling, salespeople draw out the client's thoughts and feelings in order to get an accurate picture of the client's current reality.

Scenarios. In the connecting stage of the learning wheel, people look for links between their past and the future they want. Scenarios, the second stage of ScenarioSelling, allows clients to try on different futures. They look at the possible results of different choices, in order to decide which one is most desirable.

Solutions. Solutions involve identifying and choosing a best-fit solution to deliver on their chosen scenario.

Action. In Action, clients perform the necessary tasks to bring their proposed solution into reality. All the client's activities are organized around implementing the game plan and getting things done.

I. Discovery: Helping Clients Tell Their Stories

The first stage of the ScenarioSelling process is Discovery—helping clients tell their stories. Completing the Discovery phase involves:
- Gathering the Facts (what you know)
- Drawing out Assumptions (what you don't know)
- Clarifying Concerns and Desires
- Identifying Prior Experiences

Discovery draws out the past and present to give a clear picture of their *current scenario* (the current reality): an understanding of where someone stands today.

Examples of Discovery language include:
- *What do you currently have?*
- *How did you select (or choose) it?*
- *What do you like about it?*
- *What do you not like about it?*
- *Tell me more about….*
- *What led you to that view?*
- *If you could do it over again, what would you do differently?*

Why do we call this process Discovery rather than 'Interviewing' or 'Fact-Finding'? Like 'Reflection' the Discovery phase should draw out both facts and feelings. The client's story involves more than just facts (content); it reveals patterns and relationships (context) that illustrate the reasons for change and the obstacles confronting change.

Looking closely and clearly at current reality is one of the most difficult and important tasks involved in making change. It's important to see the world as it is; even it makes us feel uncomfortable because *it's hard to get where you want to go if you don't have a clear picture of where you are.*

The Discovery process helps to get truth 'on the table.' Identifying the truth involves more than facts…it includes finding out what people know, what they don't know, and what they have trouble articulating.

The transition from *Discovery* to *Scenarios* starts to take place when the focus of conversation shifts from past and present to the future. When you get past what someone knows and is sure of, and start talking about what could be, you begin the Scenario process.

II. Scenarios: Evaluating Possible Futures

Completing the Scenarios stage involves:
- Playing out Possibilities (playing out hopes and fears)
- Identifying changes that have Leverage (things that make a big difference)
- Determining Wants (moving from possibilities to choices)
- Creating a Shared Vision

Possible scenarios help you identify opportunities and challenges you may face. A good scenario session includes playing out your dreams and fears. When you play them out, it gives you a sense of (1) what can happen, (2) what may happen, and (3) what consequences could result. The purpose is to help clients determine what they truly need and want—their *preferred* scenario.

What do we mean 'helping them find what they want'? Don't people already know what they want? When it comes to complex decisions, the answer for the vast majority of people (i.e., practically everyone) is NO! What people *want* is directly related to what they think they can have (what they think is possible). When dealing with complex problems people struggle with balancing the possibilities until they play them out.

When it comes to complex problems and decisions, people generally do not know what they want or how to articulate it until they *see it.* When they do see it, an almost magical moment takes place that can explained by the **Principle of Creative Tension** (see page 207).

How do you choose between the possible scenarios you've considered? When you're running scenarios, it's inevitable that there will be one or two that the client liked best. After you've played through a variety of options, ask the client to tell you which ones they would like to see again. Now, begin to drill down into it and refine it based on the prospect's interests and concerns.

Examples of Scenario Language:

- *Let's look at your current scenario.*
- *What happens if you do nothing?*
- *Are you willing to accept this outcome?*
- *What would you like to change about this?*
- *Would you like to see what would happen if we changed _____?*
- *Would you like to see what you could have?*
- *Let's see what would happen if disaster struck.*
- *What does disaster mean to you?*
- *Now that you've seen what's possible, what looked best to you?*
- *Let's go back to the scenario you liked best.*
- *Tell me what you like about it?*
- *What questions do you have about it?*
- *Is there anything you would like to change about this or added to it?*
- *(To others in room in multiple prospect sales) What would you do differently?*

Playing out scenarios helps answer the question, "What do you *really* want?" The work accomplished in Scenarios is just what some clients need. Once they identify their real wants and needs, they move into action, sometimes too quickly. They need the kind of direction that comes from developing goals and weighing alternatives to achieve thoughtful and appropriate action. The next stage, Solutions, describes the work involved in doing this.

III. Solutions: Developing Goals and Plans

In *Discovery* & *Scenarios* phases, you developed pictures of where you are and where you want to go. *Solutions* closes the gap between these two. In the Solutions stage, you determine what you need to do or obtain to get what you want.

The *Solutions* stage has four parts:

- Creating Goals (objective statements of the desired end result)
- Establishing Priorities (what are you willing to give up to get what you want?)
- Evaluating Alternative Strategies (what do you need to do or get to achieve your goals?)
- Making Choices (what alternatives are most appropriate given your goals, priorities, and options?)

Sales advisors add value in the Solutions stage by helping clients create goals and develop formal plans to accomplish these goals. Goals are specific statements about what clients want and need. The principle is clear: goals increase problem and solution clarity. Clarity increases the probability of success.

Strategy is the art of identifying and choosing realistic courses of action for achieving goals and doing so under adverse conditions. Planning is the process of developing strategies. While the value of helping clients set goals is obvious, practical goals and plans do not usually leap out fully formed. They need to be shaped.

Professional planning suggests (requires) a high level of skills, discipline, and experience. Effective advisors add value by using their communication and problem solving skills and experience to shape goals and plans.

Solutions language includes:

- *Now that you know where you want to go, let's find out how to get you there.*
- *Let's start by turning these dreams into goals.*
- *Goals are dreams with deadlines.*
- *If you could only accomplish one of your goals which would you pick?*
- *Let's look at some alternatives to help accomplish this goal.*
- *Let's consider the costs and benefits of those alternatives.*
- *What tradeoffs are you willing to make?*
- *What types of choices have other people made in your situation?*
- *What choices or options do you think/feel fit you best?*

The Solutions stage results in a plan. But planning should not be confused with action. Without action, goals and plans are nothing more than wishful thinking. The ultimate test of their effectiveness lies in the results they produce. The next and final phase of the ScenarioSelling process describes what's required for results-producing action.

IV. Action: Making It All Happen

In the *Solutions* stage, you create the plan. In the *Action* stage, you work the plan. Action describes the tasks and other steps needed to turn goals and plans into results.

The Action stage involves:

- *Tactics*—Helping clients turn strategies into tactics: What do I need to do first? What do I need to do second? Etc.
- *Monitoring*—Setting benchmarks to determine whether someone is on track or whether changes are necessary; knowing when to implement next steps and follow-up plans
- *Logistics*—Knowing how to adjust when inevitable changes occur; planning for recovery (how to overcoming setbacks); endurance (the resilience to see a plan to completion); putting systems in place to deal with post-decision regret and to help sustain changes; having a backup plan
- *Renewal*—Knowing when it's appropriate to start the cycle over; repeating the sales cycle process as appropriate

Examples of Action language include:

- *Achieving goals always starts out by taking a few small steps.*
- *Let's take a look at what you should do first/second.*
- *All changes involve some period of adjustment.*
- *Let's set some benchmarks so that you'll know when changes may be required.*
- *Periodically we'll review your wants and goals to determine if any changes are required.*

Planning plays a key role in implementation because it helps clients understand why and how to persevere when the relationship between actions and results is not intuitively obvious (for example, when long term benefits have short term costs).

Clients who set goals and start down a path to accomplishing them have taken a significant step. Implementation isn't just the end of the sales process. It's the beginning of another problem-solving and decision making (learning) cycle.

In review, the picture and table below provide a summary of the ScenarioSelling process described in this chapter.

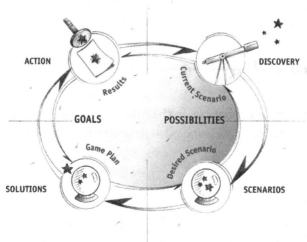

Part	I. Discovery	II. Scenarios	III. Solutions	IV. Action
1	Facts	Possibilities	Goals	Tactics
2	Assumptions	Leverage	Priorities	Monitoring
3	Concerns	Wants	Alternatives	Logistics
4	Experiences	Shared Vision	Choices/Decisions	Renewal
Outcome	*Current Scenario*	*Desired Scenario*	*Game Plan*	*Results*

The next two sections describe what makes this process *dramatically* different than other sales methods and why it works so effectively to motivate people to action.

What's Different? Possibilities Come Before Goals!

ScenarioSelling turns the traditional sales process inside out:
- Instead of starting with client goals and developing possibilities to achieve them...
- It starts with evaluating possibilities and then choosing among them to determine goals. [15.2]

Scenario planning puts possibility planning before goal planning because it is not always possible to set goals before evaluating possible solutions. Usually, goals evolve and change naturally throughout the scenario planning process. When a person goes through the scenario process, they begin to see more clearly what they want and what they have to do to get it.

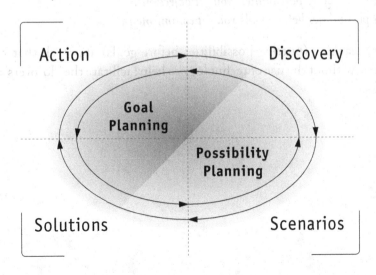

Consultative and transactional selling models are goal-based. The needs identification stage of consultative selling presumes the existence of a known and desirable goal(s)...which is great if people know what they want. But most people don't really know what they want (goals) until they know what they can have (possibilities).

This is particularly true when faced with complex problems and decisions. That's why when you're dealing with complex client issues, goal-based planning approaches don't work and even interfere in the decision/sales process.

It's a sales training cliché that objections are merely requests for more information. But it's also commonly taught that the requests surface as salespeople attempt to close the sale because they didn't provide enough information earlier in the sales process.

However, going back, or regression, is a necessary part of learning. Objections are often a client's way of bringing up new possibilities. In a step-based model, going back is considered a failure—the result of missing a step—instead of a natural part of the learning and decision-making process.

With the Scenario Sales method, those 'what ifs' can be explored as they surface. 'Objections' aren't handled at the end of the process; they're part of it. They're the fuel to accelerate the decision process.

By the time most clients have chosen a solution, they've explored so many options and have had so many anxieties addressed, the 'objections' have taken care of themselves.

Exploring those options before asking people to set goals and plans to achieve them is what sets ScenarioSelling apart.

When you're dealing with complex issues...
- *If you put goals before possibilities, you get objections.*
- *If you put possibilities before goals you get commitment.*

The discovery learning (putting possibilities before goals) approach that we are describing wouldn't be possible without the use of technology to help facilitate the 'do-overs' that are a natural part of the process.

Why Does It Work So Effectively: Creative Tension!

What causes people to make decisions rather than put them off? What motivates people to take action rather than settle for what they currently have? The answers to these questions can be found in *the principle of creative tension*. Creative tension[15.3] is a term popularized by leading thinkers in the subject of change management to explain what motivates people to change.

Creative tension describes the feeling people have when they recognize the difference (the *gap*) between where they are (their *current scenario*) and where they want to be (their *preferred scenario*). The 'gap' is the distance between what we have and what we want. This gap creates a natural and healthy tension that seeks to resolve itself. This tension is the reason choices are made and actions are taken. It's the source of energy for change.

Creative tension is a natural force. Have you ever seen how lightning works? You can't see it, but as the poles become charged ionized particles between the poles begin to 'line up.' When the forces at the poles are strong enough—zap—a powerful spark bridges the gap. Let's see how this applies to *decision-making* and *selling*.

Decision-Making & Creative Tension. When people see something they want, there is a natural tendency to move toward it. This power (creative tension) pulls us toward our vision. It's a very powerful motivator. What is motivation? Motivation is a 'need.' It is an internal drive that requires action. Motivation is like the volume on the radio. It describes the level of intensity dedicated to resolving an issue. The stronger the tension, the greater the motivation, and the more likely that change will result.

Once you know what you want in relation to what you have, you begin to organize your thoughts and actions, consciously and unconsciously, to cause the desired change to happen. Creative tension is an innate pull that seeks resolution; and the most natural resolution of this tension is for our reality to move closer to what we want.

Selling & Creative Tension. Sales efforts that don't recognize and address the natural forces at work typically collapse into 'pushing' the prospect towards the salesperson's vision of what the client wants. Sales efforts that utilize creative tension 'pull' prospects and clients towards the vision that they themselves have created.

How do you use the concept of creative tension in a sales situation?
- Provide a clear picture of where they stand today
- Develop a shared vision of what they want

If you do a good job on these two points, the natural impact of creative tension will introduce a 'productive discomfort' that will cause the client to seek resolution. As a result, they will buy rather than having to be sold.

In the next chapter, we describe the Knowledge, Skills, and Tools this requires.

KNOWLEDGE, SKILLS, AND
TOOLS REQUIRED

"If you can't explain it to a six year old, you don't understand it yourself."
—Albert Einstein

ScenarioSelling integrates all stages of the sales cycle to eliminate unnecessary delays and provide a seamless process flow between prospecting, interviewing, presenting, managing objections, and closing. ScenarioSelling uses technology to help clients and salespeople evaluate possibilities, make decisions, and take actions faster and more effectively.

Despite the advantages, we know that there are many salespeople and companies who will struggle to do this…for four basic reasons:

(1) They haven't had the right tools to do it (what they use)

(2) It requires different methods (how they use the tools)

(3) It requires different skills and training (what they already know and do)

(4) It goes against many of the 'rules' of the current paradigm for professional selling (why they do it this way)

To sell collaboratively with customers in real time (do it now), new tools, new methods, and new skills are required…supported by a new way of thinking.

New Thinking Required?

Let's start by looking at the hardest part—getting people to think differently. Not customers... but salespeople. There will be many salespeople who either can't or won't be able to do this because it will force them to do things differently.

Consider what we're suggesting? Doing things faster...integrating technology into the process... making changes in front of people. The ideas we're proposing challenge many of the institutionalized myths of selling.

Old Myths	New Realities
The best way to solve hard problems is to break them into parts.	Complex problems are big picture issues that can't be broken into parts. They have to be solved as wholes.
When it comes to selling, high-touch and high-tech are opposites and incompatible.	Technology and personal touch are only opposites if you're using technology wrong.
The more time you spend with someone, the greater value you add.	When a customer's time is valuable, you create greater value by taking less of it.
Making mistakes in front of a client is bad and should be avoided.	Making mistakes is part of learning. The ability to recover determines good from bad.
Quality takes time. Fast means cheap.	Quality is not the result of time. It's the result of an effective process. Extra steps that add time decrease quality.
Building trust takes time.	Trust can be built quickly if you provide an environment for people to take risks safely.

It accomplishes this using the same proven principles that American manufacturing and service industries have used to increase productivity and quality through *process improvement*...[16.1]

Just-in-Time...
Simulation Modeling...
Scenario Planning...
Lean Thinking...
Six Sigma...

People will continue to struggle to understand these changes and the new behaviors required until they begin to think about these issues differently. How do you do this?

New Thinking. In the Appendix, we provide the outline for a college course that describes the learning objectives for this new approach.

New Tools. New thinking is often introduced by tools that provide us with new and better ways to work.

We believe the following quote from Buckminster Fuller helps illustrate the point.

"If you want people to think differently, don't bother trying to teach them. Give them a tool, the use of which will lead to different ways of thinking."

To get people to think differently about selling, we need to look at the tools involved in each stage of the sales process.

Tools/Equipment Needed

ScenarioSelling is done visually and interactively. All steps are completed with the customer. What type of tools are required to do this? *Tools designed for visual interactive collaboration!*

Advances in digital technology in the last 10 years have paved the way for this type of approach. Some of the technologies used to do this weren't available or easily affordable as recently as a few years ago.

We're going to suggest three choices that represent *Basic*, *Better*, and *Best* options. Each of these cases involves a computer with a monitor or viewable screen. The differences are screen size and position.

Basic. A 'Basic' choice is to use a laptop with a large screen (15") or better. In this scenario, people huddle around the computer and try to look at it together. When is this appropriate? It works best when there are very few people involved. As you add people, a small screen is less practical and valuable.

Better. A 'Better' choice involves putting the screen between the people. This suggests using a larger screen, like a 19-30" monitor.

Best. The 'Best' choice involves using a large screen. This can be accomplished by using a computer with a multimedia projector or a large screen TV.

Why is Bigger Better?

Attention. It's much easier to pay attention. The smaller the image, the harder it is to stay focused. With a big picture, it's harder NOT to pay attention.

Comfort. The laptop and projector combination make it possible for all participants to look comfortably and easily at the same picture.

Experience. The difference in experience is dramatic. Consider the differences between watching a movie on a 12" screen, a large screen TV, or at an IMAX theatre. It's not just a different physical experience; it's a different emotional experience.

The collaborative ScenarioSelling process is more than a passive movie experience. It's like being in an audience participation movie.

But hardware alone is not enough to promote effective collaboration. Simply putting a tool between the participants is not enough. What you're looking at—the software or visual medium—is just as important.

Software Needed

Real collaboration occurs with neither the frequency nor the intensity it should, because there are few tools explicitly designed to encourage it. At a minimum, we suggest the software you use must be *visual* and *interactive*.

What Do We Mean by Visual? Colorful and graphic...software that looks like television rather than data tables and spreadsheets.

What Do We Mean by Interactive? Interactive tools are designed to allow changes in inputs. The degree of interactivity can be measured by the ease of changes and the speed of response. The easier it is to make changes and the faster the response, the more interactive it is.

Decision Flight Simulators! What do visual interactive real-time planning tools look like? Think 'flight simulators'. What would it look like if you built a 'flight simulator' for customer decisions? A few industries have implemented tools that demonstrate promise.

Medical. Plastic surgeons, for example, use software programs that show patients the possible outcomes of surgical procedures. Together doctors and patients choose the products and services most appropriate to the patient's needs.

Financial Services. We developed a program called RetireNow as a financial flight simulator to help financial advisors and consumers evaluate possible outcomes of retirement and estate planning decisions. Together advisors and clients identify needs and goals, and then co-create solutions to resolve them. It's like trying on financial solutions before you buy them!

Let's suppose for a moment that you had the right tools for visual interactive simulation with customers. Is that enough? *No.* That's because collaboration requires more than just hardware and software; it requires additional skills and knowledge.

Skills Needed

Collaborative environments have to be created. Success at collaboration depends on your ability to engage other people in the process, not simply on your ability to perform or persuade. Technology-based collaborative selling requires competency in three skills sets: *selling, planning,* and using *technology* …and the ability to do them at the same time.

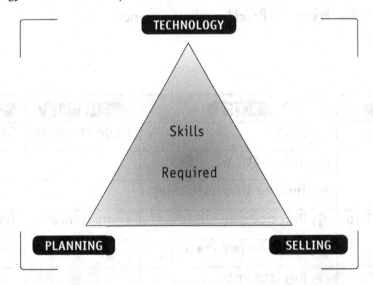

Technology (Inputting and manipulating the data). Technology skills include: The ability to use a computer, how to run the specific software program you need, and how to set up and use multimedia equipment. You have to be able to get the data into a computer program, manipulate, and present it.

Planning (Interpreting the information). When you put data into a software program, what do you do with the information it spits back? Many people fail to sell effectively with technology because they don't know how to interpret or use the information provided by the software program.

Selling (Dialoguing about it). Selling skills involve knowing how to ask questions and facilitate a process that leads to appropriate action. Selling requires the ability to engage in productive problem-solving dialogue. Talking may be a natural skill to some salespeople, but dialoguing is a trained skill.

Achieving a Balance. Planning, selling, and using technology at the same time can be a fairly challenging juggling act. Most salespeople don't have the skills and experience needed in all three areas to pull it off. You don't have to be an expert in all three, but you have to have functional skills in all of them.

Additional training is usually required to build the skills and knowledge necessary for this type of approach. This doesn't mean you can't sell if you don't have these skills. It just means that it will be harder to do it well.

Training Model. Here's a grid we use to illustrate how to achieve sales mastery through a professional development program that includes: Education, Training, and Coaching.

Selling as Learning: Process + Practice + Performance

PLACE	TACTICS	OBJECTIVES	PROCESS
Class Room	1 Study	Understanding	Education
	2 Observation		
	3 Testing Understanding		
Practice Field	1 Practice	Competence	Training
	2 Practice Feedback		
	3 Adjustments		
Playing Field	1 Field Performance	Mastery	Coaching
	2 Performance Feedback		
	3 Adjustments		
	4 Evaluate the Process		

The model and the graphic help illustrate four important key points about Sales Learning:

1. Learning to sell is not an event that happens in a classroom. It's an ongoing process of achieving Understanding, Competence, and Mastery in selling.
2. A Sales Learning model is designed to help people progress along the path to sales mastery, by integrating Education, Training, and Coaching.
3. A Sales Learning approach accelerates learning and selling providing better skills development and sales results.
4. ScenarioSelling requires skills in three separate areas: selling, planning, and using technology.

It's not often that you find all of these skills (selling, planning, and using technology) in one person. So how do you implement it? What alternatives are there to help make this possible and practical?

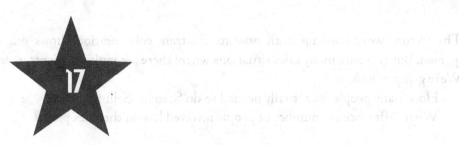

IMPLEMENTATION—
THREE SCENARIOS

In the last few chapters, we defined ScenarioSelling, we outlined the activities involved, and we discussed the knowledge, skills, and tools required. In this chapter, we're going to describe how it's implemented.

Let's start with a basic question: How many people does it take to do ScenarioSelling?

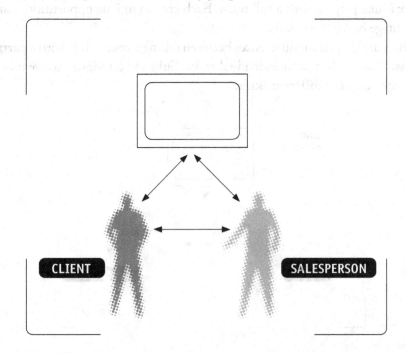

The picture we've used up until now to illustrate collaboration shows one client and one salesperson. But there are many sales situations where there are multiple clients or sellers involved.

We're going to look at:

♦ How many people are actually needed to do ScenarioSelling?
♦ What difference the number of people involved has on the sales process?

As a result, we'll provide a framework to understand what's required for effective individual and team-selling situations.

Solo, Sulu, or Sandbox?

Here are three scenarios[17.1] that describe different ways ScenarioSelling can take place. Each involves a different number of salespeople:

♦ *Solo:* One Salesperson (working alone)
♦ *Sulu:* Two Salespeople (a partner approach)
♦ *Sandbox:* Three or More Salespeople (a team approach)

All three are collaborative approaches. What's the difference between them? Consider the difference in sports, for example: basketball. Selling **Solo** is like playing 1 on 1. **Sulu** is like playing 2 on 2. **Sandbox** is like playing with a full team. Each creates unique opportunities and challenges. Each takes advantage of different skills.

Likewise, there are significant differences between selling alone, selling with a partner, and 'team' selling situations. Solo involves more individual tasks. Sulu and Sandbox involve more group tasks. And as a result, each requires different skills.

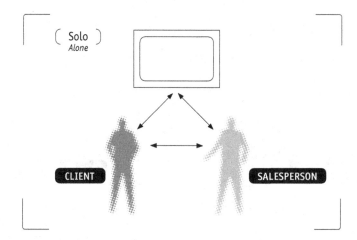

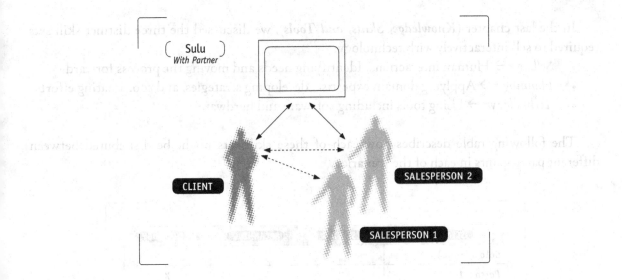

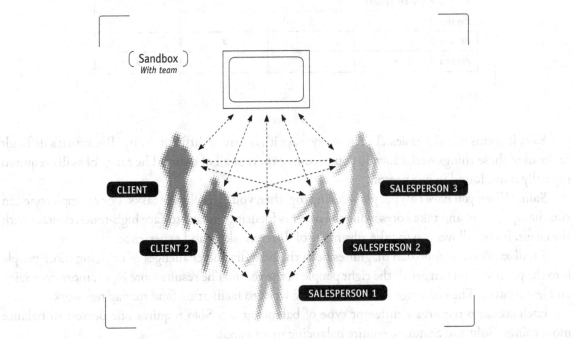

Different Skills Required

In the last chapter (*Knowledge, Skills, and Tools*), we discussed the three distinct skill sets required to sell interactively with technology:

- *Selling* $\longrightarrow$ Human interactions. Identifying needs and moving the process forward
- *Planning* $\longrightarrow$ Applying domain expertise, developing strategies, and coordinating efforts
- *Technology* $\longrightarrow$ Using tools including software and hardware

The following table describes how each of these skill sets might be distributed between different participants in each of the scenarios.

SCENARIO	SELLING	PLANNING	TECHNOLOGY
Solo (Alone)			
Person 1	X	X	X
Sulu (With Partner)			
Person 1	X	X	
Person 2		X	X
Sandbox (With Team)			
Person 1	X		
Person 2		X	
Person 3			X

Solo. It seems like the easiest, but in many ways it's the most difficult. Why? Because it's difficult to do all of these things well. How do you become expert at all of them? The range of skills required typically is not found in one person.

Sulu. When you have two people working together, you can split the tasks. For example, one can run the equipment and take notes while the other is focusing on face-to-face high-touch contact with the client. It also allows you to take advantage of different skills and experience.

Sandbox. A team approach magnifies both the benefits and challenges of bringing more people into the process. You can get all the right people in the room. The result: more input, more creativity, and less control. The challenge shifts from doing work to facilitating (and managing) work.

Each scenario requires a different type of balancing act. Solo requires one person to balance more things. Sulu and Sandbox require balancing more people.

When Is Each Appropriate?

When is each appropriate? Is it simply a matter of preference? Remember the goals: helping people solve problems and make decisions.

Choosing the appropriate scenario depends on: the problem being solved, the resources required to resolve it, and the skills of the people involved.

When trying to determine which is best for your situation, use the following table as a guide.

SCENARIO	BENEFITS	CHALLENGES	SKILLS
Solo (*Alone*)	Greater Control Less people involved	More skills required less personal	Individual Skills
Sulu (*With Partner*)	Leverage different skills More personal	Less control	Facilitation Skills
Sandbox (*With Team*)	Greater collaboration creativity Bring all the decision makers and resources together	Even less control	Leadership Skills

Suggestions for Getting Started

Here are some suggestions for getting started:

1. Start out by tag-teaming with another person (*Sulu*).
2. Progress to *Solo* as you develop mastery of the different individual skill sets.
3. Progress to *Sandbox* based on mastery of facilitation and team skill sets.

The advantage of starting Sulu (or with a partner) is that you don't have to have mastery of all the skills or how to coordinate them. It often works well to coordinate efforts between a person who focuses on the technology and another who focuses on the clients. It also helps you take advantage of the development and mentoring opportunities of pairing an 'old pro' with a young technician.

If you do go **Solo,** don't start out by trying it on your most important prospect. Do it in situations where you can feel reasonably comfortable fumbling and making mistakes. For example, annual reviews with current clients. Another way to start is to use it simply as an interview approach.

As for **Sandbox**…you bring the most resources possible and all the decision-makers together. But coordination can be difficult. Remember this is a team approach. There are few things as beautiful to watch as a team that plays well together. Likewise, there are few things as awkward or frustrating to watch as a disorganized or unprepared team.

Practice. To accelerate your skills, consider these practice methods:

- Use it as a method for discussing proposals at sales meetings
- Use it as a case-study style training approach

Just do it! The biggest obstacle to effective ScenarioSelling isn't the client's, it's the salesperson's. Salespeople are afraid of making mistakes in front of customers. But if you're a little bit awkward in using technology, people generally don't notice or care. In fact, it feels more genuine and objective than a slick controlled sales presentation.

The sooner you can get to doing this in front of customers, the more effective you will find the ScenarioSelling process.

SCENARIOSELLING SUMMARY

"Learning is not compulsory…neither is survival."
—W. Edwards Deming

In this final chapter, we replay the core themes of the book. This provides a summary which may be useful to pull together the many separate and interdependent parts which make up the ScenarioSelling concept. It may also be valuable as a "quick start" guide.

Death of the Salesman?

There is increasing pressure for all parties to a sale to prove their value or be eliminated. Some experts make compelling arguments that we don't need salespeople at all. The Internet provides a 24-hour storefront and customer service access. Many sales positions have been eliminated as companies reduce or de-emphasize their sales force in favor of technology-based alternative channels, particularly the Internet.

Technology and Selling

Technology will not replace all salespeople, but it will continue to replace many sales functions and change the way that salespeople create value.

Why Consultative Selling Must Be Surpassed

It's increasingly true that professional selling involves planning. (You're either planning or you're pitching.) The current paradigm for professional selling, consultative selling, doesn't easily accommodate the use of technological planning tools in the sales process. Attempts to integrate the two end up causing delays, providing a poor customer experience, and killing sales. There must be a better way.

Fast-Professional Selling Is No Longer a Paradox

Conventional selling suggests that selling is either fast and impersonal or slow and professional. Competitive pressures and consumer expectations demand that we find a way to bridge the gap. If professional selling is going to survive it must evolve to become both fast and professional. But how?

Many people equate selling faster with high-pressure/less professional selling. We've talked to many professionals who said, "I can't do it faster. It'll make it look too easy. They'll think I don't do anything." This is particularly true of and difficult for sales consultants and advisors who bill for their time.

Some salespeople are concerned that performing the sales process start to finish faster might make customers think that they are not receiving the best possible service or product...that the salespersons value is directly related to time. But one of the paradigm shifting rules of the Digital Age is that value creation is now *inversely related* to the time involved.

The manufacturing world got a rude awakening on this subject in the 1980s. The quality movement proved that this is not true. In fact, adding time can lead to increased errors and reduced quality, resulting in a less effective and more costly process for all involved.

Just-in-Time Methods and Tools

Fast-professional selling can be accomplished through the application of lean thinking (just-in-time) principles and tool. When you integrate technology into professional selling, you do more than simply add tools. You fundamentally change the process. Professional selling in the future must become *technology-based* to bridge the fast-professional divide.

Reengineering Is Required

This requires reengineering both the methods and tools of selling. Re-engineering is a process that requires us to start over. When we start over with selling, what principles do we base our new model on?

Selling as a Social Science

We have to start out by defining what selling is. To provide selling the legitimacy it deserves we based it on our definition of scientific principles. We view selling as a social science, like psychology, economics, and management science. It's a helping profession in which professional helpers (salespeople) work with consumers to help them solve problems and make decisions. What types of problems do people need help with that require the assistance of professional helpers?

The TOP (Type of Problem) Model

Problems can be broken down into four basic types based on the amount of information and experience required to solve them. The four types are: Simple, Complicated, Complex, and Hyper-Complex. The types of problems/decisions where human helpers provide the greatest value are 'experiential'—complex and hyper-complex problems. What's required to understand and solve these problems?

The Relationship Between Goals and Possibilities

You can't put goals before possibilities when people don't know what they want. When you're dealing with complex problems, people don't know what they want!

Complexity and Selling

Technological advances reduce (or replace) the value that salespeople provide for most types of problems. Most salespeople don't have the knowledge, tools, and skills to help clients solve complex problems.

It's difficult (and maybe impossible) to replace the role of human helpers when people are trying to solve highly complex problems. ScenarioSelling represents the only type of sales problem-solving model where people cannot be replaced by technology.

A Learning Approach

Traditional linear (strategic) problem solving tactics are ineffective when trying to solve complex problems. A learning approach is required. ScenarioSelling changes selling from a seller-directed (teaching) process to a buyer-directed (learning) process. Selling is a learning process for both the buyer and the seller. Selling requires a buying decision to take place. Decision-making is the result of a learning process. The types of problems that clients need a salesperson's help with require a collaborative learning approach.

Seller as Buying Facilitator

How does the seller's role change when we redefine selling as a learning process? A collaborative learning approach to selling changes the salesperson's role from expert resource (seller as consultant or teacher) to expert facilitator. Fulfilling this new role requires new knowledge, skills, and tools.

Knowledge and Skills Required

A collaborative learner-centered approach to selling may look unstructured, but requires a higher level of skill and preparation than a teacher-directed approach to selling. It requires understanding of and belief in the process.

Tools Required = Decision Flight Simulators

Collaboration requires a shared space between the buyer and seller—a place for them to work, make changes, and create together. Interactive multimedia tools like computers and projectors provide an ideal medium for collaboration. Collaboration with multimedia technologies turns the sales process into a session of visual interactive play, not child's play, but serious play. Decision Flight Simulators describes a new class of tools designed to help clients and advisors work together during a planning-selling process.

Improving the Customer's Sales Experience

Collaborative play redefines the customer sales experience. In the increasingly competitive global marketplace, there is no place for sales processes or people that make buying difficult or painful for consumers. Buying/selling methods that make the process engaging, enticing, and entertaining will have a distinct advantage over those that don't.

ScenarioSelling Principles

ScenarioSelling has the following characteristics:
1. Done Just-in-Time.
2. Uses computer technology.
3. Uses simulation.
4. Done in front of customer.
5. Solves a complex or hyper-complex, systems problem.
6. Uses possibility planning, not goal-based planning.
7. Incorporates customer in any necessary analysis of situation.

Accelerating Trust

It is true that time can build trust. But it is not true that trust takes time. It's a matter of misperception regarding what comes first—the feeling of trust or the act of trusting. Trust can be built stronger and faster with the proper application of E.S.P. (Environment, Skills, and Process).

Why ScenarioSelling Is Inevitable

Given the pace and volume of change, learning is the key to staying competitive for both individuals and organizations. The biggest challenge today is not getting an education, it's keeping one. We need to keep updating our knowledge and skills throughout our entire working lives.

To succeed today, all businesses and their employees must continually reshape themselves, shift, and flex to fit a rapidly changing world. They must adapt, adjust, and adopt new technologies and procedures.

Why ScenarioSelling Is Imperative

Technological advances are changing the way people create value. Salespeople must adapt and evolve if they are to survive. Professional selling has evolved from consultative to collaborative.

'Selling to' is out. 'Selling with' is in. Salespeople need new knowledge, skills, and tools to make this transition.

ScenarioSelling describes the theory, methods, and tools required to collaborate effectively with customers. It redefines the role of the salesperson and the skills required to survive and thrive in the Digital Age.

Are you ready to make the investment?

AFTERWARD

PROPOSED SCENARIOSELLING
COLLEGE COURSE

We have included the following outline designed to facilitate a senior or MBA level college course on ScenarioSelling. We have additional materials including model projects, homework assignments, and other materials you will see referenced in the outline.

If you are interested in teaching this course, please email us at: president@scenarionow.com.

COURSE:	Advanced Sales Seminar (Technology & Selling)
COURSE NUMBER:	Marketing 400 or 500 Level Class
SECTIONS:	1 & 2
CLASS TIME:	
Section 1:	T 1:00-3:00 PM
Section 2:	T 3:00-5:00 PM
PROFESSORS:	Your Name
OFFICE:	Your Office
OFFICE HOURS:	To Be Determined
OFFICE PHONE:	Your Phone
E-MAIL:	Your Email

Course Overview

Can technological advances eliminate the need for salespeople? Technological advances in the last 20 years have had a dramatic impact on almost all areas of business and society. In this course, we'll study the impact of technology on selling. Participants in this course will gain an understanding and appreciation of the technologies (theories + methods + tools) required to survive and thrive in the Digital Age.

Professional sales training programs have an obligation to prepare trainees for the tasks and responsibilities of the sales profession. This not only involves theory, methods, and tools appropriate for selling today, but preparation for environmental and technological changes that will shape the future of the profession.

This course is based on a scientist-practitioner model of professional sales with the following beliefs:

- Sales is a discipline with a core set of technologies: theories + methods + tools.
- When a sales practitioner appropriately applies these, value is created for the customer, the company, and the salesperson.
- Changes in technology change the way that value is created, and therefore have a direct impact on the value of selling and salespeople.
- A sales professional is a practitioner who understands and uses research evidence to validate their sales models and change them when appropriate.

This rigorous course draws on leading theory and best practices from several different disciplines including information systems, manufacturing, marketing, psychology, and education.

Prerequisites

- *Prior sales experience/training:* An understanding of consultative selling process is assumed. Marketing 3XX or experience equivalent is required.
- *Technology experience/training:* Participants must have access to a computer. Basic skills in word processing software, presentation software (i.e., PowerPoint), and using the Internet to perform research are assumed.
- *A willingness to be influenced:* Some of the ideas proposed in this class will violate current conventional wisdom and many of selling's sacred cows. An open mind is required.
- *Participation:* This is a professional sales course. Active participation is a critical part of the learning process and is expected.

Required Texts

1. <u>ScenarioSelling: Technology and the Future of Professional Selling</u>, Patrick J. Sullivan and Dr. David L. Lazenby, (Trafford Publishing, 2005).
2. <u>ScenarioSelling Workbook: Case Studies and Exercises</u>, Sullivan & Lazenby, (Scenario Publications, 2005).
3. <u>The Fifth Discipline Fieldbook: Strategies and Tools for Building a Learning Organization</u>, Senge, Kleiner, Roberts, Ross, and Smith (New York, NY: Currency/Doubleday, 1994).

Course Objectives

1. To identify the history of selling as related to production, marketing, and sales.
2. Draw a model of sales process pipeline.
3. Explain the differences between the processes and activities of marketing, selling, and servicing.
4. Define and differentiate the terms suspect, prospect, customer, and client.
5. Define technology's role in value creation in the Digital Age.
6. Identify the skills required to effectively integrate technology into the sales process.
7. Define and recognize case examples of the difference between problem solving and decision making.
8. Identify the selling process with the problem types.
9. Understand shared space and its role in collaboration.
10. Identify the baseline skills required for technology-based selling.
11. Explain the impact of technology on the evolving role of the salesperson.
12. Describe different types of forecasting methods and their appropriate use.
13. Explain the challenges of using goal-based planning under conditions of uncertainty.
14. Explain what is meant by 'planning as learning.'
15. Explain what is meant by 'selling as learning.'
16. Illustrate and describe the challenges of integrating technology with a traditional consultative selling process.
17. Define re-engineering and provide two industry examples.
18. Explain what is meant by reengineering the sales process.
19. Describe the four types of selling.
20. Compare and contrast consultative and collaborative sales approaches.
21. Draw and describe the DSSA Model.

22. Define Systems Thinking and describe the elements of a systems diagram.
23. Define and provide examples of the appropriate use of archetypes and BOT graphs.
24. Explain the concept of creative tension and its relevance to the sales process.
25. Describe why simulation is usually required for systems thinking.
26. Describe the relationship between simulation and scenario planning.
27. Identify the key drivers needed to create a decision flight simulator.
28. Describe the four roles of the salesperson and their relationship to computer technologies.
29. Illustrate the Learning Wheel. Describe the appropriate transfer of each stage to selling and decision-making.
30. Define and describe VIPS.
31. Define 'trust' and demonstrate two examples of how technology can accelerate trust.
32. Use the NERVES Model to describe how to capture and keep a customer's attention.
33. Identify your personal 'people pattern' and describe its influence on your sales strengths and weaknesses.
34. Define/describe Interactive Multimedia, including the equipment and software involved.
35. Be able to differentiate between synchronous and asynchronous media and their appropriate uses.
36. Illustrate and describe the three models for collaborative selling (individual and team). Be able to develop your own definitions of these three models.
37. Describe CRM—what it is and its relationship to the sales process.
38. Provide examples of appropriate uses for technology in marketing, selling, and servicing.
39. Explain what is meant by the Experience Economy and provide two industry examples of how value is created for the buyer in this economy.
40. Explain the three metrics for fast professional selling and provide an example of each in action.

Note: While most of the learning objectives and topics described in the list above are covered in the ScenarioSelling book and workbook, some are not. Information regarding availability and licensing of these additional materials can be found at www.scenarioselling.com or by contacting the authors.

Suggested Course Outline

WK	TOPICS	READINGS	PROJECTS and HW DUE
1	Introduction: Selling—Past, Present, and Future	What Is Selling Anyway? Selling—Event or Process? From Suspects to Clients— The Sales Process Pipeline Death of the Salesman? The History of Selling The Evolving Role of the Salesperson	HW #1: Pre-class survey
2	Technology & Selling	What Is Technology? Technology and Value Creation Sales Tools— From the Stone Age to the Digital Age Being Digital Selling—The Fast Professional Paradox Technology Disabled Consultative Selling	HW #2:
3	Reengineering the Sales Process	What Is Reengineering? Real Time: The Need for Speed In Search of Muda Selling—A Technology-Based Approach Just-In-Time Professional Selling	Project #1

4	Problem Solving & Decision Making	What's Your Problem?—
		    Identifying Problem Types
		Problem Solving vs. Decision Making
		Managing Complexity
		Decision Making Under Uncertainty
		Non-linear Decision Models
		The Four Types of Selling
		Matching Selling & Problem/
		    Decision Types
			HW #3

5	**EXAM 1—CONCEPTS FROM WEEKS 1-4**		

WK	TOPICS	READINGS	PROJECTS and HW DUE
6	The Discipline of Collaboration: Theory, Methods, and Tools	What is Collaboration? Communication vs. Collaboration Why Collaboration? How Do You Collaborate? Shared Space Collaboration as Serious Play	HW #4
7	Part I—Theory: Intro to Systems Thinking	What Are Systems? Why Systems Thinking? Balancing the Short Run and the Long Run Modeling Complex Problems Loops, Archetypes, and BOT Graphs The Learning Journey	Project #2
8	Part II—Methods: Intro to Scenario Planning	Comparing Forecasting Methods What's the Goal—Precision or Accuracy? The Perfect Information Myth Planning as Learning Mental Models The Learning Wheel Discovery Based Learning	HW #5
9	Part III—Tools: Intro to Simulation	What Is Simulation? Why Simulation Is Required for Systems Thinking The Relationship Between Simulation and Scenario Planning Decision Flight Simulators™ Learning—Simulate to Accelerate VIPS—Visual Interactive Planning & Selling™	HW #6
10	EXAM 2–CONCEPTS FROM WEEKS 6–9		

WK	TOPICS	READINGS	PROJECTS and HW DUE
11	Selling—A Learning Model	ScenarioSelling™—Selling as Learning The DSSA™ Model Understanding Creative Tension Technology-Based Discovery Creating a Shared Vision From Collaboration to Commitment Empowerment— The Capacity for Effective Action	Project #3
12	Human Technology (Skills Required)	Counselor 101: The Helping Process Helping Skills: PEARLS™ Know Your Customer: Recognizing People Patterns Accelerating Trust From Blatant to Latent— Identifying Real Needs The FIND Formula™ Navigating Through Complexity Balancing Hopes and Fears	HW #7
13	Computing Technologies	Interactive Multimedia Hardware—What's Required? Software Design and Selection Solo, Sulu, or Sandbox?: Models for Individual and Team Selling CRM—The Promise, The Failure, and the Future	HW #8
14	The 21st Century Salesperson	Surviving and Thriving in the Digital Age Selling—The Final Frontier The Experience Economy New Sales Metrics— Redefining ROA, ROE, and ROI The Scenario Imperative	Project #4
15	EXAM 3-CONCEPTS FROM WEEKS 11-14		

BIBLIOGRAPHY/
RECOMMENDED READING

Aldrich, Clark. Simulations and the Future of Learning: An Innovative (and Perhaps Revolutionary) Approach to e-Learning. New York: Pfeifer Publishing Group, 2003.

Basalla, George. The Evolution of Technology. Cambridge, MA: Cambridge University Press, 1990.

Cooper, Alan. The Inmates Are Running the Asylum: Why High Tech Products Drive Us Crazy and How to Restore the Sanity. Indianapolis: Sams Publishing, 1999.

Courtney, Hugh, Jane Kirkland, and Patrick Viguerie. Harvard Business Review on Managing Uncertainty. Cambridge: Harvard Business School Press, 1999.

Covey, Stephen. The Seven Habits of Highly Effective People. New York: Fireside Publishing, 1989

Davis, Stanley M. Future Perfect. Reading, MA: Addison Wesley Press, 1987.

De Geus, Arie P. "Scenario Planning: Planning as Learning". Harvard Business Review. Mar-Apr 1988. 70-74.

Downes, Larry and Chunka Mui. Unleashing the Killer App: Digital Strategies for Market Dominance. Cambridge: Harvard Business School Press, 2000.

Egan, Gerald. The Skilled Helper: A Problem Management and Opportunity Development Approach to Helping. New York: Brooks/Cole, 2002.

Gates, Bill. The Road Ahead. New York: Penguin Books, 1996.

Gee, James Paul. What Video Games Have to Teach Us About Learning and Literacy. New York: Palgrave Macmillan, 2003.

Goldratt, Eliyahu. The Goal: A Process of Ongoing Improvement. Great Barrington, MA: North River Press, 1992.

Hammer, Michael. Beyond Reengineering: How the Process Centered Organization Is Changing Our Work and Our Lives. New York: Harper Collins Publishing, 1996

Heijden, Kees van der. Scenarios: The Art of Strategic Conversation. New York: John Wiley & Sons, 1996.

Keirsey, David. Please Understand Me (Volumes I & II). Del Mar, CA: Prometheus Nemesis Book Co Inc., 1998.

Martin, Iris. From Couch to Corporation: Becoming a Successful Corporate Therapist. New York: John Wiley & Son Inc., 1996.

Meyer, Christopher. Fast Cycle Time: How to Align Purpose, Strategy, and Structure for Speed. New York: Simon & Schuster Inc., 1993.

Montgomery, Steven. People Patterns: A Modern Guide to the Four Temperaments. Geneva, NY: Archer Publications, 2002.

Negroponte, Nicholas. Being Digital. New York: Random House Inc., 1995.

Pande, Peter, Robert Neuman, and Roland Cavanagh. The Six Sigma Way Team Fieldbook: An Implementation Guide for Process Improvement Teams. New York: McGraw Hill, 2002.

Peppers, Don and Martha Rogers. The One to One Future: Building Relationships One Customer at a Time. New York: Bantam Doubleday Dell Publishing, 1993.

Pine, Joseph and James Gilmore. The Experience Economy: Work Is Theatre and Every Business a Stage. Boston: Harvard Business School Press, 1999.

—. Markets of One: Creating Customer-Unique Value through Mass Customization Boston: Harvard Business School Publishing, 1998.

—. Mass Customization: The New Frontier of Business Competition. Boston: Harvard Business School Publishing, 1993.

Schein, Edgar. <u>Process Consultation: Volume I</u>. New York: Addison-Wesley, 1998.

—. <u>Process Consultation Revisited: Building the Helping Relationship</u>. New York: Addison-Wesley, 1998.

Schrage, Michael. <u>No More Teams: Mastering the Dynamics of Creative Collaboration</u>. New York: Bantam Doubleday Dell Publishing, 1990.

—. <u>Serious Play: How the Worlds Best Companies Simulate to Innovate</u>. Boston: Harvard Business School Publishing, 1999.

Schwartz, Peter. <u>The Art of the Long View: Planning for the Future in an Uncertain World</u>. New York: Doubleday Dell Publishing Group Inc., 1991

Senge, Peter. <u>The Fifth Discipline: The Art and Practice of the Learning Organization</u>. New York: Bantam & Doubleday Dell Publishing, 1990.

Senge, Peter, Art Kleiner, Charlotte Roberts, Richard Ross, and Bryan Smith. <u>The Fifth Discipline Fieldbook: Strategies and Tools for Building a Learning Organization</u>. New York: Currency/Doubleday, 1994.

Simon, Herbert. <u>Models of Bounded Rationality, Vol. 3: Empirically Grounded Economic Reason</u>. Cambridge: MIT Press, 1997.

Sterman, John. <u>Business Dynamics: Systems Thinking and Modeling for a Complex World</u>. New York: McGraw Hill Publishing, 2000.

Tapscott, Donald. <u>The Digital Economy: Promise and Peril In The Age of Networked Intelligence</u>. New York: McGraw Hill Publishing, 1996.

—. <u>Growing Up Digital: The Rise of the Net Generation</u>. New York: McGraw Hill Publishing, 1998.

<u>The Systems Thinker</u>. Ed. Colleen P. Lannon and Daniel H. Kim. Waltham, MA: Pegasus Communications

Tufte, Edward. <u>Visual Explanations: Images and Quantities, Evidence and Narrative</u>. Cheshire, CT: Graphics Press, 1997.

Waldrop, Mitchell. <u>Complexity: The Emerging Science at the Edge of Order and Chaos</u>. New York: Touchstone Publishing, 1992.

Womack, James and Daniel Jones. <u>Lean Thinking: Banish Waste and Create Wealth in Your Corporation</u>. New York: Simon & Schuster Inc., 1996.

NOTES

ScenarioSelling is the result of a collaboration that blended two worlds: sales practice and psychology. Together, our efforts have resulted in a model for a professional sales-psychologist. In doing so, we've blended practice and theory to create a new sales model built on scientific principles.

At first we struggled to find resources to help us because there is very little science to the practice of selling. What we did find was 'practitioner' grade, not 'professional' grade. So, we looked to other disciplines. Since 1996, we have read hundreds of books and articles from several different fields including selling, psychology, learning, management, and technology to help frame and advance the social science of selling.

As a result, the ideas and methods in this book owe a great deal to authors and consultants whose work in these areas enlightened, inspired, and challenged us. In particular, we are indebted to the following people whose research and writing helped provide the structure and language to express our thinking.

- To Peter Senge and associates for the 5th Discipline books. Thanks for helping us understand how to think systemically and to become better learners.
- To Nicholas Negroponte, Donald Tapscott, and others who helped us understand what it means to 'Be Digital' and open our minds to the implications of the Digital Age for individuals and businesses.
- To Joseph Pine and James Gilmore for providing the depth and detail to advance the concepts of Mass Customization and the Experience Economy from cocktail conversation to professional practice.
- To Don Peppers and Martha Rogers for providing the language and thinking for CRM and helping us understand what a 1:1 Future could look like.
- To Ron Willingham, who helped us understand how to look at sales training as an ongoing learning process rather than a series of discontinuous educational events.
- To Michael Hammer for demonstrating how to create 'first principles' to apply scientific thinking to social sciences like management (and selling); and for helping us understand

the connection between processes and value.

- To James Womack and Daniel Jones for helping us understand how to build a process around lean principles that eliminate *muda* (waste) and create greater value.

- To Mitchell Aldous for helping us understand the relationship between order, chaos, and complexity.

- To Peter Schwartz for helping us understand how to use scenario planning to think forward more effectively.

- To Arie deGues for writing the article (Scenario Planning: Planning as Learning) that inspired the name of this book.

- To John Sterman for helping us see the link between Systems Thinking and Simulation and how to use simulation to counter bias, avoid jumping to conclusions, and provide a clearer picture of both reality and possibilities.

- To Herbert Simon, whose life and work provided the inspiration for dividing sales problems into different types; and helping us understand the difference between problem-solving and decision-making.

- To Michael Schrage for helping us understand the concept of shared space, why it's required for collaboration, and how to use simulation to promote deeper discovery. His works will forever change (for the better) the way that people work and solve problems *together*.

- To Gerald Egan for providing structure and depth to the professional counselor model and for showing us the skills and methods necessary for salespeople to become 'skilled helpers'.

- And to countless consultants and practitioners who have dedicated their careers to the sales profession.

In the remainder of this section, we provide notes and references for each chapter of the book.

  *   *Books, articles, and other reference sources in the following pages are mentioned by author and title only. More complete information on sources, including publisher and date, is provided in the Bibliography/Recommended Reading section on pages 239-241.*

Chapter 1: Death of the Salesman?

Chapter 1 forms the thesis of the book—that salespeople must adapt the way they work and create value or be left behind by a world that finds them irrelevant and unnecessary.

In the 1990s, a number of books hit the stands professing that new technologies would change the way that businesses create value, therefore eliminating many middlemen, including salespeople.

- In <u>Being Digital</u>, Nicholas Negroponte describes how digital technology produces profound and fundamental changes in our world today. In his view, we are experiencing a watershed event, where digital technology will lead us on to a new age.
- Donald Tapscott's <u>The Digital Economy</u> furthers this thinking, explaining how industries will converge and how many middlemen will disappear. He also openly wonders if new technologies will eliminate the need for salespeople.

Our View: In fact, many sales positions have been eliminated as companies reduce or de-emphasize their sales force in favor of technological alternatives, particularly those that are Internet-based. However, we don't think that all sales-middlemen will necessarily be erased by new technology. Rather, we believe they will evolve as new tools transform their jobs and how they perform them.

Other key influences to this chapter included:

- Tapscott, Donald. <u>Growing Up Digital: The Rise of the Net Generation</u>
- Davis, Stanley. <u>Future Perfect</u>
- Downes, Larry and Chunka Mui. <u>Unleashing the Killer App: Digital Strategies for Market Dominance</u>

Chapter 2: The Modern History of Selling

Chapter 2 provides a model to help us understand the business problems and solutions posed by advances in technology. In particular, it illustrates that we have entered a new age which requires salespeople to evolve beyond the current paradigm of consultative selling. The shared-history model we created comparing how new technology led changes in production, marketing, and selling was influenced by several books, particularly: <u>Mass Customization</u> by Joseph Pine and James Gilmour; and <u>The One to One Future</u> by Don Peppers and Martha Rogers. The idea for the final piece to the puzzle came while driving and listening to a tape of Tom Siebel speaking at a sales force automation conference in Chicago, in March of 1999.

(2.1) Pine, Joseph and James Gilmore. <u>Mass Customization: The New Frontier of Business Competition</u>

(2.2) The terms we use to describe consultative selling are a synthesis of several programs we like, particularly Ron Willingham's <u>Integrity Selling</u>. We think Ron captures the true essence of the consultative selling/training *process*.

(2.3) EOQ is a production management term meaning Economically Optimal Quantity. It is used to determine *batch-size*: the amount of a product which should be made to take advantage of production efficiencies without creating excessive inventory. The history of production in the 20th Century illustrates a fascinating story of how EOQ/batch-size got smaller and smaller as new technologies and processes made it both possible and practical.

(2.4) From Bill Gates book, <u>The Road Ahead</u>

(2.5) Davis, Stanley. <u>Future Perfect</u>

(2.6) Pine, Joseph and James Gilmore. <u>Mass Customization: The New Frontier of Business Competition</u>

(2.7) Peppers, Don and Martha Rogers. <u>The One to One Future: Building Relationships One Customer at a Time</u>

Other key influences to this chapter included:

• Basalla, George. <u>The Evolution of Technology</u>

Chapter 3: Consultative Selling and Technology: A Tale of Woe

In this chapter we explain the challenges posed when you try to integrate consultative selling methods with new digital age tools. Some of the things we say can be construed to mean that we don't like consultative selling. In fact, we like it very much. But it is our belief that the Digital Age requires salespeople to evolve to develop new processes, skills, and tools.

(3.1) We illustrate the sales process on an engineering project-management Gantt chart to illustrate the steps, the order in which they occur, and time required for each. The Gantt chart concept is valuable because it allows us to demonstrate potential sources of delay in the sales process.

(3.2) Egan, Gerald. <u>The Skilled Helper</u>

(3.3) This direct reference from page 97 of <u>The Experience Economy</u> by Joseph Pine and James Gilmore helps illustrate one of the key themes of this book. Improving the sales process isn't simply for companies…it's for customers. Companies must improve the customer sales experience if they want to compete in the 'Experience Economy'.

(3.4) This note was graciously provided to us by George Dudley, President of Behavioral Sciences Research Press. Text on page 93 from: George W. Dudley; permission to cite/reproduce in Scenario Selling Technology and the Future of Personal Selling (textbook only); November 2004. Internal reference #3 from: Chonko, L., Tanner, J., and George W. Dudley, "Differential Diagnosis of Sales Call Reluctance", 50th Annual Convention, Southwestern Psychological Association, San Antonio, Texas.

Other key influences to this chapter included:

• Cooper, Alan. <u>The Inmates Are Running the Asylum: Why High Tech Products Drive Us Crazy and How to Restore the Sanity</u>

Chapter 4: Selling-The Next Generation

Chapter 4 brings the previous chapters to their logical conclusion—there will be a new sales process in the Digital Age that will surpass consultative selling. It introduces the dilemma that results from trying to reconcile dueling demands of selling professionally and selling faster. The story that results builds a bridge to Part III of the book where we attempt to analyze and resolve the fast-professional paradox.

(4.1) Time-share is a term we came up with to help explain the value of shortening the sales cycle (selling faster). In learning how to overcome these limits we benefited greatly from the ideas in Chris Meyer's Fast Cycle Time.

(4.2) Sell fast or sell professionally? This paradox of conventional sales wisdom is not resolved by either transactional or consultative selling. This dilemma is the result of limits to thinking that imply that you can only do things in either a transactional way or consultative way. To help understand these dilemmas and how to think about them differently we learned a great deal from Eliyahu Goldratt's The Goal: A Process of Ongoing Improvement.

(4.3) Another invaluable resource for learning how to improve process efficiency, effectiveness, and quality is Lean Thinking: Banish Waste and Create Wealth in Your Corporation, by James Womack and Daniel Jones.

Chapter 5: Building a New Foundation

If we want to achieve fast-professional selling, the traditional selling methods must be "broken" and then "rebuilt". This chapter goes through the process of explaining how to re-engineer and rebuild selling scientifically.

(5.1) The major influence of this chapter was Michael Hammer's book Beyond Reengineering: How the Process Centered Organization Is Changing Our Work and Our Lives.

(5.2) Simon, Herbert. Models of Bounded Rationality, Vol. 3: Empirically Grounded Economic Reason

(5.3) The definitions of decision science, psychology, economics, and management science are compilations from many different resources including college texts and technical dictionaries.

(5.4) Here we take the concepts of a chapter of Beyond Reengineering titled, "What is Business Anyway?", and illustrate their applicability to selling. The idea was to provide a framework for establishing selling as a social science.

Chapter 6: What's Your Problem?

Chapter Six provides a framework for understanding the different types of problems clients face. This chapter builds on Chapter Five's conclusion that the value created by sales people is directly related to the type of problem the client wants/needs to resolve.

(6.1) TOP is an acronym for the <u>T</u>ype <u>o</u>f <u>P</u>roblem Model, which we created to describe four distinct problem 'classes' or types.

(6.2) The definitions and model for Certainty, Risk, and Uncertainty come from pages 12-37 <u>Games and Decisions</u>, by R. Duncan Luce and Howard Raiffa. This book discusses how individual decision making is framed by game theory.

(6.3) The definitions for the terms *complicated* and *complex* came from synthesizing several dictionary and technical resources. We were particularly sensitive to clarifying the differences while maintaining the integrity of their historical roots.

(6.4) *Hyper-complex* is a term used in mathematics and science to describe shapes with more than three dimensions. As a result they are difficult for people to understand and explain without appropriate modeling tools and metaphors.

Other key influences to this chapter included:

- Bernstein, Peter. <u>Against the Gods: The Remarkable Story of Risk</u>
- <u>Harvard Business Review on Managing Uncertainty</u> (The Harvard Business Review Paperback Series)

Chapter 7: Understanding Complexity

The concept of complexity is so vital to our story that we decided to dedicate one entire chapter to the subject. Chapter 7 attempts to clarify what complexity is and the challenges complexity creates for selling. We've included a list of the "Laws of Complex Selling" and an explanation of the relationship between complexity and sales objections.

Chapter references and ideas were drawn from:

(7.1) Senge, Peter. <u>The Fifth Discipline: The Art and Practice of the Learning Organization</u>

(7.2) Waldrop, Mitchell. <u>Complexity: The Emerging Science at the Edge of Order and Chaos</u>

Chapter 8: Managing Complexity

Chapter 8 explains three subjects that help people better understand and manage complexity: systems thinking, simulation, and scenario planning. It also illustrates the linkage between them. In summary: (a) systems-thinking makes understanding complexity *possible*; (b) simulation makes systems thinking *practical*; and that (c) scenario planning makes simulation *purposeful*.

(8.1) Systems Thinking resources include:
- Senge, Peter. The Fifth Discipline: The Art and Practice of the Learning Organization
- The Systems Thinking Workbook. by Systems Thinking Press

(8.2) Simulation Resources include:
- Schrage, Michael. Serious Play: How the Worlds Best Companies Simulate to Innovate
- An article in the Fifth Discipline Fieldbook, by MIT professor John Sterman explaining "Why Simulation Is Required for Systems Thinking"

(8.3) Scenario Planning resources include:
- The Art of the Long View by Peter Schwartz
- Heijden, Kees van der. Scenarios: The Art of Strategic Conversation

Chapter 9: The Role of Human Helpers in Problem Solving

Chapter Nine describes the different roles people (human helpers) play when helping other people solve problems. This chapter illustrates how different helper roles are related to the four types of problems identified in the TOP Model.

(9.1) We felt the quote from Harvard's Chris Argyris was an appropriate introduction to this chapter since it points out the need for 'others' to help point out systemic structure. In other words, people play a key role in helping others recognize how systems (complex) problems work through feedback.

(9.2) The language of helping came from two primary resources: the research and experience of Dr. David Lazenby; and The Skilled Helper, by Gerald Egan. The Skilled Helper is a highly respected and widely used textbook for training graduate students in psychology. We feel that it's language and methods play a critical role in helping professionalize the helping process for salespeople.

(9.3) The language of collaboration owes much to the work of Michael Schrage's work, particularly the books Serious Play and No More Teams.

(9.4) Schrage, Michael. No More Teams: Mastering the Dynamics of Creative Collaboration, notes summarized from various pages.

Chapter 10: When Are Salespeople Necessary?

Chapter Ten applies the language and helper roles defined in the prior chapter to selling. This helps illustrate what types of problems require sales helpers. The table describes the four types of selling and relates them to the problem types identified in the TOP Model.

Chapter 11: Technology and Selling Reconsidered

Chapter Eleven revisits the relationship between technology and selling and brings closure to Part III of the book. The chapter and Part III conclude with the affirmation that there are some types of selling where both people and technology are required.

(11.1) The Schrage quote reflects on the change in thinking required in the application of technology to selling. A shift must take place from using technology to providing a medium to facilitate relationships.

(11.2) What differentiates 'technology-enabled' from 'technology-based' selling? It's a difference in design. The language is borrowed from the computer software industry and parallels the difference web-enabled and web-based software: two different approaches to software design.

Chapter 12: From Consultative to Collaborative

Chapter Twelve differentiates the process of consultation from collaboration, and describes the different types of technology appropriate for each. This helps clarify the differences between consultative selling and collaborative selling and the process required for each.

(12.1) The depth of language and thinking regarding collaboration in this chapter benefits from the books listed below:

• Schrage, Michael. <u>No More Teams: Mastering the Dynamics of Creative Collaboration</u>
• Schrage, Michael. <u>Serious Play: How the Worlds Best Companies Simulate to Innovate</u>

Chapter 13: A Learning Approach

Chapter 13 describes what learning is and explains the relationship between learning and selling. It builds on earlier discussions that regarding the value of a learning-approach when dealing with complex problems and issues. We provide an illustration of what a learning approach to selling might look like. The relationship between learning and complexity suggests an understanding of the concept of regression (taking steps back before you can move forward). Our coverage of this subject is based on several psychology textbooks and the experience of Dr. Lazenby. The chapter ends with a discussion of the application of accelerated learning principles to selling.

(13.1) De Geus, Arie P., *Scenario Planning: Planning as Learning* (article)

(13.2) The idea that companies (and salespeople) create value through learning relationships was introduced to us by Don Peppers and Martha Rogers The One to One Future.

(13.3) The learning wheel is a concept attributed to Charles Handy, which describes the stages and the cycle people go through as they learn. Our discussion of the subject is based on pages 59-64 of The Fifth Discipline.

(13.4) The link between learning and selling suggests that principles of accelerated learning should help us understand how to accelerate the sales process. The 12 Guiding Principles of Accelerated Learning (and selling) are ours.

Chapter 14: Accelerating Trust

The relationship between trust and speed in the sales process is discussed in Chapter 14. The key point is that selling faster doesn't require building more trust up front, if trust is built as a result of the sales process. Most sales processes are trust 'taxing' rather than trust building processes. Chapter 14 covers how to create a trust building sales process.

References:

(14.1) Senge, Peter. The Dance of Change: The Challenges to Sustaining Momentum in Learning Organizations

(14.2) Covey, Stephen. The Seven Habits of Highly Effective People

Chapter 15: The ScenarioSelling Model

Chapter 15 introduces the ScenarioSelling Model: a picture of the ScenarioSelling process. The ScenarioSelling process originated and evolved in the field as a result of actual client experiences. The model came about as we worked to validate these experiences with scientific principles. In short, the development process involved bending the sales steps into a circle, and then applying scenario-learning concepts and language.

Our thinking in this process was strongly influenced by Gerald Egan's book, The Skilled Helper: A Problem Management and Opportunity Development Approach to Helping. In it, Egan illustrates the four-stage process a psychologist goes through as they work with clients. In our opinion, professional selling is also a process of problem management and opportunity development. As a result, Egan's work is very valuable to help understand what's required to become a professional helper.

There are two critical points at the end of the chapter that help explain (a) what makes ScenarioSelling different and (b) why it works so effectively.

(15.1) *What makes ScenarioSelling different?* It's possibility-based, not goal-based: possibilities come before goals. The idea of placing possibilities before goals, while new to selling, is one of the features of scenario planning that distinguishes it from other types of planning. Our discussion of possibilities and scenario planning benefited greatly from:

- Peter Schwartz's <u>The Art of the Long View: Planning for the Future in an Uncertain World</u>
- Two books by Kees Van Der Heijden, <u>The Sixth Sense: Accelerate Organizational Learning with Scenarios;</u> and <u>Scenarios: The Art of Strategic Conversation</u>

(15.2) *What makes ScenarioSelling work so effectively?* The discussion of *creative tension* is based on our interpretation of Kurt Lewin's Force Field Analysis.

A little background:

- Kurt Lewin (1890-1947) is considered one of the pioneers and founding figures of psychology, group dynamics, and organizational development.
- Force Field Analysis is a method for analyzing change that provides a framework for looking at the factors (forces) that are either driving movement toward a goal (helping forces) or blocking movement toward a goal (hindering forces).
- It is a considered a significant contribution to the fields of organizational development, process management, and change management.

We believe the creative tension concept provides a valuable framework for the scenario planning process and illustrates why scenario planning is such an effective way to facilitate change.

Chapter 16: Knowledge, Skills, and Tools Required

Chapter 16 describes what's required to *do* ScenarioSelling. It provides an overview of the knowledge, skills, and tools needed to apply the ScenarioSelling process.

The major influences for this chapter are:

- <u>Lean Thinking</u> by James Womack and Daniel Jones
- Peter Senge's book, <u>The Fifth Discipline</u>
- Research and experiences associated with our consulting practice

(16.1) <u>Lean Thinking</u> describes a way of thinking and working to help eliminate the delays and waste that get in the way of giving a customer what they want…when they want it. The customer-driven process flow model that results explains what's required to deliver products/ services JIT.

(16.2) <u>The Fifth Discipline</u> is an excellent resource that touches on many of the subjects in ScenarioSelling including: learning theory, systems thinking, scenario planning, microworlds, and simulation tools. <u>The Fifth Discipline</u> also clearly illustrates that mastery of a learning discipline is a developmental process. This played a role in the development of our ETC Sales Mastery Model. (ETC = Education + Training + Coaching.)

As we've worked with companies to provide training for ScenarioSelling we found companies at various levels of knowledge, experience, and readiness in the subjects discussed. We developed the ETC Sales Mastery Model to provide a developmental framework for the education, training, and coaching we believe are necessary to understand, apply, and master this sales method.

We developed the college course outline referred to in this chapter (and included in the appendix) as a result of discussions with several university business schools. It is intended to provide a more rigorous academic look at the subjects included in this book.

Chapter 17: Implementation-Three Scenarios

Chapter 17 describes three different implementation scenarios for ScenarioSelling (Solo, Sulu, and Sandbox) each referring to the number of people involved in the process.

Which of these three scenarios is the best approach? We suggest that it depends on several factors, particularly the skills of the salespeople involved and the requirements of the client situation. Some client problems and sales situations require people of different and complementary skill sets to be involved.

We close the chapter with the suggestion...*just start*. We believe that much of what you learn from this book will be the result of applying its principles in selling situations.

(17.1)   The terms Solo and Sandbox refer to implementation scenarios that involve one salesperson (Solo) and many sales team members (Sandbox). The term Sulu describes a two person or partner sales approach. The name is based on a character in the original Star-Trek television show. Lieutenant Hikaru Sulu is the helmsman of the USS Enterprise. It is Sulu who actually runs the controls and flies the ship, under the direction of Captain Kirk.

Picture two salespeople working together...one acting as the 'captain' focusing on the client...the other acting as Sulu and running the sales technology. Together they navigate the client through difficult problems and decisions.

As an interesting footnote, in a later Star Trek movie, Sulu gets promoted to captain and gets his own ship (Star Trek VI). Likewise, it is easy to imagine that in selling, the sales 'helmsman' at the technology controls could grow and transition into a 'captain' or lead sales role. This has implications for development of a sales mentoring program which we intend to write more about in future articles.

INDEX

ABOUT THE AUTHORS

Patrick J. Sullivan, MBA is CEO of ScenarioNow Inc. He has an MBA in Financial Planning and 18 years of production, marketing, sales, and management experience in the insurance, banking, and pharmaceutical industries. Mr. Sullivan has extensive experience in sales training and expert skills in software development, project management, and use. He is the author of ScenarioNow Inc.'s RetireNow™ and WealthScenarios™ software programs: visual interactive planning (VIP) tools designed for financial service sales professionals.

Dr. David L Lazenby, PhD is President of ScenarioNow Inc. He is a licensed psychologist with a PhD in performance psychology. Dr. Lazenby has guided Fortune 100 executives, professional athletes, sales professionals, leaders of privately held businesses, and U.S. Navy SEALs and pilots for over 15 years. His mission: fine-tuning their already exceptional performance. Dr. Lazenby is an expert in simulation, systems thinking, and scenario planning who works to take psychology from academic theory to the real world as a "human technology."